The First 15

The Morning Routine that Took me from Barely Surviving to Livin' the Dream!

www.MattScoletti.com

Livin the Dream Publishing

Pittsburgh, PA

For information, address Livin the Dream Publishing at livinthedream@outlook.com.

Cover designed by Karen Captline of BetterBe Creative

Edited and Formatted by Cori Wamsley at CoriWamsley.com

Printed in the United States of America

Library of Congress Cataloging-in-Publication Data

Scoletti, Matt.

The First 15: The Morning Routine that Took me from Barely Surviving to Livin' the Dream!/ Matt Scoletti.

ISBN: 978-1718952133

Livin the Dream Publishing

Thank You

My wife, aka Chef Steph

My mom, dad, and brother

Chris Johnson (On Target Living Family!)

Toastmasters International

Tony Robbins

Zig Ziglar

Table of Contents

Introduction

"We are what we repeatedly do. Excellence, then, is not an act, but a habit."

~ Aristotle

Welcome! You made it! You found the book that will help you conquer the first 15 minutes of your day! Now you only have to worry about the other 23 hours and 45 minutes right?

Seriously, if you learn to conquer the first 15 minutes of each day, then your day, week, month, and life will improve tremendously.

My name is Matt Scoletti, and I'm a certified health coach, personal trainer, mind/body specialist, and fitness nutrition specialist. I love life and truly believe with all my heart that every day I wake up is going to be the best day of my life! I've coached hundreds of people as a personal trainer and health coach, and I've learned that if you don't have a healthy mindset, attitude, and purpose, then the workouts and diet don't mean anything. That's why I began teaching my friends and clients about having a powerful 15-minute morning habit!

I'm proof that this morning routine can completely turn your life around. And if your life is already headed in the right direction, this book can help you conquer your next goal and make sure you are living the life that you were born to live! That was my motivation for writing this book. If a life like mine—which was an unhealthy, alcoholic, overweight nightmare—could be transformed, then I feel compelled to share how it was done and help others with their journey. The morning habit I developed is a problem-solving routine to help fix issues with health, mindset, attitude, or other aspects of your life that you want to improve.

This isn't a "quit your job today and chase your dreams" book. It is a book that teaches you to create and upgrade your current habits to live up to your potential! This book is designed to help you lead the most fulfilled life possible no matter your job, family, or financial circumstances. I changed my entire perspective of myself and on life while having the same 9-5 job the entire time. I've coached countless people who have changed their lives without making a job or career change. (However, if you decide that a job or career change is the right move for you, then go after what you want!)

This book is designed to motivate, empower, excite, and help you break through fears, barriers, and limitations that you have put on yourself. The morning routine I developed has helped people who were overweight, feeling depressed, heavy smokers, felt stuck in life, or just needed guidance on how to improve the quality of their lives and make them feel more fulfilled. This routine has improved the lives of people in their teens and 20s as well as retirees and every age in between!

Many of the individuals I've worked with have told me that when their first 15 minutes is productive, it makes other tasks throughout the day much easier to complete! My hope is that you will feel the same way and difficult tasks become easier in your day-to-day life.

As Aristotle said, "we are what we repeatedly do," and we become what our habits are. It makes sense. If you have a habit of brushing and flossing your teeth twice a day, then you'll probably avoid cavities or having gum problems. However, if you only brush or floss every so often, and don't make it a habit, then you are likely to have some teeth issues later in life.

The same goes for your First 15 routine. If you have a motivating, exciting, inspired, fun first 15 minutes of your day, then the rest of your day will reflect that morning energy. Once this morning routine becomes a habit, your life will have more meaning, and you'll feel much more fulfilled. However, if you only do your morning routine 1-2 times a week or a couple times a month and then quit, then you'll likely have some mental cavities that'll hold you back from living the life you truly desire. This routine—or your custom morning ritual—must be completed a minimum of 5 days a week for it to become a habit and be the most effective for you.

My driving force behind writing this book is to help you squeeze the most out of your time on this planet! I want you to wake up and live each day with purpose! My goal is to help you live life on YOUR TERMS and have a fulfilled life full of health, energy, and happiness. The days of you waking up groggy with your only goal being "make it through the day" are over! Life is too short to live like that, and living each day with purpose has to start with a strong morning routine.

It took me almost a decade to get over my struggles and begin living the life I do now. I had to write this book because I don't want anyone to go through similar struggles, and I definitely want to help change your life as quickly as possible. A decade is too long to be going in the wrong direction—or going nowhere!

Pablo Picasso once said, "The meaning of life is to find your gift. The purpose of life is to give it away." I love every quote I've put in this book, but this one had the most profound impact on me because my journey to finding my own gift was something I had to share with the world. Now I want to give that gift to you so you can give your own gift to others. You'll learn about my personal journey in this book, and you will also benefit from the strategies and processes I've outlined in the coming chapters.

You'll discover that I'm the type of person who likes doing something for myself but always craved doing something so much bigger that could benefit the masses. I hope this book helps you, your kids and grandkids, and generations to come. The concepts and strategies are timeless but also simple. I always tell people that I'm not smart enough to make things complicated, so they *must* be simple!

This book is broken into two parts. The first part of the book (Chapters 1-9) tells my story, from functional alcoholic to fitness fanatic. You will hear the stories that made me fall into a life of excessive partying, drinking, and inability to control my actions. You'll hear the struggles I went through as I fought some inner demons that even my closest friends and family didn't know about. Then, you'll hear about how I fought back against myself and the unhealthy lifestyle I had adopted and how I tried to overcome my fears and limiting beliefs.

The one major way I changed my life, my health, and my confidence, was by adopting this morning routine that I've worked to perfect since I started it. As you'll see, the morning routine continuously changed as I completed each event on my healthy living journey and learned more about what was important in my life. My journey helped me conquer my physical, mental, emotional, and social health. But I don't just describe what I went through. I provide sound strategies you can implement immediately after completing this book to begin *your* journey to becoming the strongest, healthiest, most confident, happy, and motivated version of you possible!

Whenever a new practice is introduced in a chapter, I explain at the end of the chapter how to execute that new practice and how it will benefit you. I also discuss all the activities in detail in Section 2 of the book.

Following the "Current First 15," you'll see an "Analysis" of my morning routine at that point in my life from my current mindset. I encourage you to use this book as a guideline for your own morning routine, but customize it to what works best for you.

In addition to my stories and morning routine analysis in the first part of the book, I include numerous challenges for you, which I hope you will accept. I know you are up for some challenges, or you wouldn't be reading this book! These challenges (don't worry, they are simple and quick) will help you accelerate your personal growth!

The second half of the book (Chapters 10–21) explains why the First 15 is so powerful and an essential part of your life. It breaks down each discipline, talks about the benefits, and dives deep into how this will help you become a better person, employee, business owner, friend, or family member.

Each segment of the First 15 Routine is designed to help you feel uplifted, inspired, and energized in the morning, instead of sluggish and demotivated. First impressions mean so much in this world. Having a positive first impression of your day is no different. When you wake up and do this morning routine, you will be in a much better spirit throughout the day and be able to more easily deal with whatever life throws at you!

This book is designed to help you—

- Become more optimistic
- Implement ideas and strategies to overcome a variety of setbacks or problems
- Become more grateful for the life you have
- Enjoy all those amazing people in your life
- Find your true self, and find the person who's been hiding for years, or even decades
- Remove excuses from your life and start living the life you were supposed to live
- Slowly create change in your life so you can be a healthier, happier you, one 15-minute segment at a time

Everyone has dreams. Or at some point, we all had dreams when we were younger. I want to help you dig deep and find some of those wants and needs and help you reach your true potential as a person, an employee, a parent, a member of the community, or a business owner. This book and process will help you. One simple formula in the morning can help transition you from a life of mediocrity into one of massive success, happiness, and most importantly, fulfillment.

I believe that the beginning of the day is a huge predictor of how the rest of your day will play out. Realizing that changed my life. In the tough times, I realized that my poor attitude and awful First 15 shaped my entire day, which would end up lousy and unproductive. Now, by mastering my First 15, I wake up each and every day with a newfound love for life! After you read this book and implement your own routine, I know you'll feel the same way!

Section 1

My Story & the Evolution of the First 15

Chapter 1 – The Beginning

"Success is a few simple disciplines, practiced every day; while failure is simply a few errors in judgement, repeated every day."

~ Jim Rohn

"BEEP BEEP BEEP BEEP!" My alarm clock went off at 7:20am. "Ugh, I hate getting up in the morning and going to work." "Click" I hit the snooze. Phew, another 9 minutes of high quality sleep.

"BEEP BEEP BEEP BEEP!" My alarm went off again at 7:29 am. Snooze.

"BEEP BEEP BEEP BEEP!" 7:38 am. Snooze.

"BEEP BEEP BEEP BEEP!" 7:47 am. Snooze.

"BEEP BEEP BEEP BEEP!" 7:56 am. There it was...my least favorite alarm of the five. When that one went off, I knew I had to wake up to make it to work by 9 am. However, I hit the snooze again because if I didn't do anything with my hair, barely ate any breakfast, and only washed 80% of my body in the shower, I knew I could cut out 9 minutes of my morning routine and make it to work by 9 am. Good. Snooze.

"BEEP BEEP BEEP BEEP!" 8:05 am. Oh crap! I would be late for work if I didn't get going! I threw the blankets and sheets off, shut off the alarm clock, and stubbed my toe on my desk chair as I ran to the bathroom to shower, shave, and get dressed. My head was spinning because I was so worried about being late for work, and I knew I had to push myself as hard as I could to make it by 9 am. But I would probably do the same thing again the next day. And the one after that.

When the next morning came, I snoozed the alarm at 7:20 am, 7:29 am, 7:38 am, 7:47 am, and 7:56 am, and again, I stubbed my toe on my office chair. I scarfed down some leftover chicken lo mien from the night before, spilling some on my tie. My mind raced to make sure I had on the right clothes, my hair looked halfway decent, and my socks matched my shoes. Breathing heavily, I jogged out the door and hopped in my car.

Adrenaline pounding through my veins, I weaved in and out of traffic and checked my phone every couple minutes for texts from last night. I was nervous about how perfect the commute had to be for me to make it to work at exactly 8:59 am. I even had to hit the elevator at the right time!

For the majority of my working career, I completed this painful, high anxiety, awful routine every Tuesday, Wednesday, and Thursday morning. Do you think that with an insanely stressful first 15–60 minutes of my day that I was even close to my most productive at work?

I mentioned that three mornings a week, this was my morning routine. The other four mornings were even worse. Mondays and Fridays were always terrible because I usually drank 8–10 drinks on Sunday and Thursday nights. I was in my mid-20s, living in a two-bedroom townhouse as a single man and enjoying the nightlife. In a 2013 article in the *Pittsburgh Business Times*, the headline read "Pittsburgh Tops for Most Bars per Capita," and I lived in the area (Southside) that helped Pittsburgh win this prestigious award.

Having friends who enjoyed the bar scene led me to meet other people while at bars, and eventually, my circle of friends became comprised of only people who craved being completely trashed a minimum of three nights per week. I rarely (if ever) saw any of them sober, and if I did, we would have an awkward conversation that would lead to a couple shots to get our friendship back to "normal."

This is why Monday and Friday mornings were a nightmare. These two mornings still consisted of the five-snooze plan. However, while scrambling to get ready for work on time, I also had a pounding headache, like a mini Rocky Balboa was inside my head throwing punch after punch to different parts of my skull. I'd often squint or take 3–4 Tylenol or Advil to help the painful punching. My hangovers were the worst. Then, I would eat whatever I could get my hands on, hoping that a lot of grease and Gatorade would miraculously cure my pounding headache. As I'm sure you guessed, none of this worked.

My extremely stressful commute was even worse with a massive headache. Then at work, my whole body felt uneasy, and I was usually still squinting from the pain in my head. Mentally, I was fine and able to function once I calmed down from my commute, but physically, I was so worn out and in pain.

Saturday and Sunday mornings were horrible too, though I had a reprieve from the alarm. After getting home and passing out the night before between midnight and 2 am, I would wake up between 8 am and 10 am. My first words were always, "I swear if I survive today, I'm never drinking again." I moped into the bathroom, looking at myself with droopy eyes, hunched over posture, pounding head, and a pathetic expression on my face. I cursed the good Lord for making it a sunny day outside because the brightness made my headache even worse.

I always had tentative plans to do something on a Saturday or Sunday afternoon, but I usually cancelled due to my binge drinking the night before. However, I never told anyone my secret—I was just too hungover to be able to function.

One morning I was scheduled to paint over graffiti in my neighborhood with some community members. The only way I got through that morning was by waking up at 9 am, doing 4 or 5 shots of vodka, and eating whatever junk I could get my hands on in the fridge first. The leader of the graffiti watch group, Harry, came up to me the first time I volunteered and said, "Wow! It's so nice to have a young person volunteer to help us out. Good for you! That shows that you have your priorities straight."

I smiled back at him, thinking to myself, "If he only knew that I could only get myself to do this because I am tipsy right now . . ."

Then I said, "Whatever I can do to help the community sounds like a great thing to me, Harry! I enjoy giving back!" And that was true! I *did* enjoy giving back. I wish I could have done it without drinking though. Looking back, I realize that I didn't have deep meaning or purpose in my life during these tough times, though I craved it.

I'd often joke around with Harry and he'd laugh. "Matt, you crack me up, my friend! You have so much energy and a great zest for life! Thanks for being around and helping out."

Comments like this made me happy but then very sad because I knew I was only so funny and outgoing because I was a few drinks in. At least, that's the same false story I kept telling myself. After every graffiti paint out, I had to go home and take a nap because I was entering the hungover phase of my day, even though it was only in the early afternoon.

One day, my good friend Nelson asked me to do a 10K race on a Sunday morning a few weeks after one of the graffiti paint out days, to which I said "Absolutely!" I had a month to train and thought I was ready for the race, until that morning—I had been severely intoxicated the night before. Nelson pounded on my door for 10 minutes until I finally opened the door with that same pathetic expression on my face.

He knew as soon as the door opened that I wouldn't be able to make the 10K. I can still close my eyes and picture the look on his face. He said, "Are you seriously not coming? We had this planned for a month, and I drove all the way over here. What were you doing last night, man?"

My head was pounding from my hangover, so I just shrugged and uttered, "I'm sorry, man. I don't know. It was just a wild night. I don't know what to tell you, and I feel awful."

He frowned. "You definitely don't look too good. I'll talk to you some other time."

I was losing friends who were doing healthy activities and gaining friends who loved late night parties, binge drinking, and lying around the following day.

After Nelson left, I attempted to blame my friends for my enormous hangover. I thought, "If only I didn't have those last two shots my buddies bought for me, I would have been fine." Right.

But I didn't *just* blame my friends. I remember multiple times getting down on my knees next to my bed and saying, "Dear Lord, why can't I be fun without alcohol anymore? I used to be fun in high school—fearless, full of life, and energized, and I never had a drink. Why must I drink *now* to be fun?" You know you have a problem when you run out of people to blame, so you start blaming God. I get a chuckle years later looking back on some of those "prayers." Don't worry, since then, I've apologized to God many times for blaming him for my problems. Hopefully He forgives me.

The blame was solely mine, of course. I had convinced myself that I had to drink alcohol to be myself. This story was not a true story, but I made myself believe it. Sobriety was the boring me that nobody wanted to be around. I was so much more fun when I was screaming obscenities, peeing on my own front door before going out at night, and dancing around with random women on the dance floor. What's strange, though, is that I would usually disappear after only 30 minutes of being out. I would think "this isn't fun anymore," and I'd walk home by myself to pass out.

A lot of the time, during my drunken walks, when I wasn't completely blacked out, I remember saying, "That's it. I need to get into shape because I love working out, I want to have that 6-pack I always thought about, and I'm going to do more with my life." But then, the next afternoon when my friends would text me the time they would be over to start drinking, I always got excited and figured that's what Friday and Saturday night were for. I deserved it. Have you ever said that to yourself? "You worked hard all week so now you deserve to get so drunk you forget about the work week, or your problems, or your stress." Until you wake up the next morning, of course. Is this how anyone should live?

I challenge you to think about some of the decisions you make this week and project how you will feel after these decisions. Then decide if the action is worth doing. If I had used this technique and visualized how awful I would feel the day after a night of drinking, maybe I could have made some changes sooner.

The craziest part about my lifestyle for these years was that nobody knew the problems I had going on internally. In fact, a lot of my friends and family who read this book will be surprised to know what I was going through. I held it all in. I figured if I could just sneak in drinks here and there, nobody would really notice how tipsy I was at family gatherings, or social events. Plus I was in my mid-20s, and that's what all single guys do in their mid-20s . . . right? You'll notice throughout this book that I regret not opening up sooner about the problems I was having, and I ask anyone who is having any problem to make sure to reach out to close family, friends, and/or a professional.

I was a lector at my church, but I never read sober in 5 years. Not once. I had at least 3 shots of vodka in me so I felt confident enough to read in front of hundreds of people. I thought I was showing fearlessness because I was reading in front of a large group, but deep down, I knew I was only weakening myself because I didn't have the guts to face my fears while sober. I thought if I didn't have at least a couple drinks in me, though, I'd panic and be unable to read. This was another false story that I made real because I chose to believe it. We become what we focus on, and at that time, all I thought about was how much I needed alcohol to speak in public.

To everyone observing my lifestyle from 2002–2011, I looked pretty normal. I held a steady job. I dated girls here and there that I would meet while at bars. I was always smiling and laughing while around friends and family, but it was because of this demon inside me . . . alcohol. Without it, I told myself that I didn't have confidence and couldn't be funny, and I *definitely* couldn't let anyone see that side of me. And nobody noticed this from the casual friend, to very close friends and family members. I was fighting this inner demon on my own, and it had been there for years.

Chapter 2 – Rise and Fall

"Transformation is a process, and as life happens there are tons of ups and downs. It's a journey of discovery - there are moments on mountaintops and moments in deep valleys of despair."

~Rick Warren

My life was perfect! I had just graduated high school and was one of the top students in my class. I was a four-year varsity basketball player and had a great relationship with my teachers (ok, some people call that a "suck up," I get it). I had a carefree attitude and loved everything about life, so life was giving me everything I wanted in return.

I was always smiling and laughing loudly. In fact, I won "funniest laugh" for our senior superlative in the yearbook. I loved everyone in our school from the jocks, to the goths, to the nerds and made sure I made friends with every single group. I couldn't walk down the hallway without saying "what's up" to 20–30 people.

Have you ever had the feeling that everything was perfect in your life? Even for a split second? Well, that is how *every day* of my life felt my senior year of high school. I always loved teasing the girls and joking around with them, and in turn, quite a few took a liking to me. But I didn't date or have my first kiss until my senior year. True story! I know what you are thinking: I didn't have any "game." Not true, I swear! Ok, maybe you're right. Who knows? Moving on!

I had the best and most loving family also! My friends were amazing, but family has always been my number one priority. I guess my mom and dad taught me well. I had a great relationship with my parents and a loving relationship with my brother. Well...most of the time. We were competitive with each other, but when we were put on the same team, we were completely unstoppable! Basically, family life was amazing!

My senior year, I was voted to be on the homecoming court. I remember asking my friends, "Why the heck would everyone vote for *me*?" It was a weird question, but I really wanted to know. My friends all gave a similar answer. They smiled and said, "Because you are YOU. You constantly smile and treat everyone the exact same way. You laugh and talk to everyone." Wow. But I was just being ME. I was being the Matt Scoletti that I loved to be. I wasn't trying to impress anyone. I wasn't trying to be someone I saw on TV or idolized. I was just doing the best job I could being the person who enjoyed life, made others laugh, and never took myself too seriously. It was one of the greatest feelings I've ever felt that day.

Then, college arrived. It was August of 2002, and I had just said goodbye to my parents as they drove away on that humid summer afternoon. I did a few fist pumps, followed with the happy dance because I was finally FREE! My parents, who I felt were insanely strict and didn't allow me to do much of anything growing up, were finally out of my hair, and I could explore my new home!

I looked out in front of me and saw a campus that wasn't ready for the energy, excitement, and love for life that I had. I was about to turn this place into my sanctuary. It was the University of Richmond in Virginia. This was the place I would spend the next four years of my life as a student but, more importantly, as a social butterfly meeting everyone I could and being the outgoing, fun, crazy man I was, just like in high school.

The first night away from my parents was an exciting one. That was the first night I got introduced to what college would be like for the next four years.

After that, my nights became a constant stream of beer flowing down my throat at least three nights per week. The average amount of drinks I consumed per week increased significantly with each passing year in school.

I was having a blast! This was so much better than high school where I had to check in with my parents every night and be home by 11 pm. Now I could stay out until 3 or 4 am and drink as much as I wanted, and that only helped me gain more and more friends! This was the best! Until it wasn't.

By my senior year of college, I was having at least four drinks *every night of the week*. I was a full blown alcoholic, even though I didn't know it.

I look back and joke that my blood alcohol content was higher than my GPA the majority of my four years in college. The only thing I was afraid of was not graduating. With only a few months left till graduation, I saw that I really would graduate, so the drinking got worse. Seven nights a week being drunk was my lifestyle. My senior year, I was just having fun, but I did have to put in a ton of extra work leading up to finals my last semester because I was close to failing a couple classes.

I had fully allowed college to ruin my sober social life. Have you ever had that friend that every time you see each other it's over a couple drinks? Or many drinks? And then when you get an hour sober with that individual, it's awkward because you are normally tipsy? This was how ALL of my relationships became because I had convinced myself that I couldn't function socially without alcohol. Whether that story was true, my constant reliance on alcohol to be social was a much bigger problem than I originally thought.

My advice to anyone attending college is to definitely allow yourself to have some fun, but make sure you don't NEED alcohol in your life to enjoy yourself. After four years of partying in college, I didn't think it was possible to be fun and social without being drunk. Please don't make the same mistake I did.

One morning I was walking to my job as the front desk guy at our college fitness center. I was so hungover that I brought a plastic mug full of two beers with me to help me get rid of my hangover. I left my shift that afternoon with a little beer left in my mug. As I walked back to my apartment, I drank the final sip, but it wasn't beer. It was water. "Oh my God, I took the wrong mug home!"

Three days later, during my next shift at the front desk, our manager took me aside. She said, "Hey Matt, one of our other employees took a sip of her water jug the other day and told me there was beer in it. You were the last one at the front desk before her, so why the hell were you drinking a mug of beer on your shift?"

I stared at her and tried to remain calm. I said the only logical thing I could think to say. "I'm so sorry you think it was me, but I have no idea what you are talking about. People have those jugs all over campus, and I don't think it's fair that you assumed that it had to be mine."

I looked her straight in the face and told her a lie. I'm sure she saw right through me, but she didn't fire me and just said she would be watching me extra close. This became a fun story to tell my friends, but at the time, I knew I was beginning to have a problem on my hands.

After I graduated college, I took a job selling spring break packages to college students who wanted to travel to popular vacation spots like Mexico and the Caribbean. When my friends or family members found out what I was doing, they would always say, "Wow, that Matthew is one heck of a smart man. He has to love every second of that job!"

I talked to insanely outgoing, young, wild college women all day and convinced them to buy spring break packages. But the best part was that I got to travel to one of the destinations every spring break to run all of the parties. On paper, it looks like my life couldn't get any better right? It was wild, it was fast-paced, and it was an alcohol-driven industry (which didn't help me with my drinking).

For two years, I worked in Boston for this company, barely making enough money to cover my rent and the cheapest food and alcohol on the planet. This "job" was basically an extension of college, and I still wasn't able to function in a social setting without being tipsy.

One of my low points came while I was on The University of Texas campus in Austin, talking to students about cheap spring break packages. My goal was to get people to sign up for our email list, where they could possibly win a free spring break trip the following year.

I was nervous and sweating because I wasn't used to talking to strangers while sober. When I approached one guy just to ask where the campus cafeteria was so we could hand out flyers, I got all sweaty and clammy. Then I began to shake. I couldn't even get out the sentence, "Could you tell me where the cafet..." I trailed off. "Cafeter—" "The cafeter—" I was so scared that I'd say the word "cafeteria" wrong that I couldn't say it. I was nervous because I knew I was sober. Thank goodness he finished my sentence for me. Then, he gave me a weird look and walked away.

That was probably the most anxious moment of my entire life. I was doing something so simple, yet I couldn't execute it. My heart was beating out of my chest, and I felt depressed because I wasn't fulfilled, appreciated, or even close to being a functional human being. I couldn't even form a sober sentence without feeling like I was having a panic attack. It was scary.

I couldn't handle it. I was so stressed out after just asking a student where the cafeteria was that I told my co-worker who was with me that I needed a drink. She agreed, and we went to a bar that had *famous* mixed drinks. It was only 2 pm, but I asked the lady if she could make me a double. After I drank one, I asked for another (and my coworker raised her eyebrow at me).

After I finished my two drinks (which were basically four drinks), my co-worker said, "Do you feel better?" I felt a little buzzed by then, so I said "Yes, I'm ready to talk to people now!" *I'm ready to talk to people now?* I wasn't comfortable talking to people without a drink (or four)? Shortly after this trip to The University of Texas—and a couple more bad experiences with this spring break company—I figured it was time to move back to Pittsburgh, Pa., my hometown.

So I did. I took a 9–5 job in the business world . . . and I bought a row house in the neighborhood with the most bars, called Southside. I had already developed my snooze-dependent lifestyle during my spring break salesman job, so it continued. Nothing was going to change it. Unless I changed myself.

At this point in my life, my morning routine was so unproductive that I hesitate to even call it a "routine." That almost acknowledges that it has structure and makes it sound professional, which clearly it doesn't deserve. It only consisted of me rolling around in my bed dreading the fact that I *should* wake up but couldn't. I wasn't quite ready to change this "routine" yet, though.

*****

Current First 15:

15 minutes – (after 4–5 snooze buttons) Moaning and groaning about the day and about how terrible I felt while I showered, jammed food down my throat, and ran to my car.

Analysis: Do I even need to analyze this? No. It needs work. We can leave it at that. And I did this same routine for almost a decade? C'mon Matt.

Chapter 3 – Breaking Point

"All truths are easy to understand once they are discovered; the point is to discover them."

~ Galileo Galilei

Have you ever taken inventory of your life? Who are your friends? What do you love about life? What are your challenges? What could you work on? I challenge you to take inventory of your life at least every six months. In fact, I'd take 5–10 minutes right now and answer those questions. You'll learn so much about yourself and the patterns you have in your life. That way, should you want to change a habit, you'll easily be able to notice which habits need changed if you want to succeed in a certain area.

Here's what I found out when I took inventory of my life one day. I was a 27-year-old man, single, owned my own house, held a steady job, had a wonderful family, laughed constantly and looked like someone who "had it all." Those are all definitely major things to be grateful for! But there was more to the story.

Despite looking like I had it all, I was completely empty inside and had no idea who I was, what I wanted from the world, or what I should be doing with myself. As you know, I was a basketball player in high school, and even though I drank a lot over the last 10 years, I loved lifting weights and went to the gym at least four nights a week. I was 5'8" and about 215 pounds. And in case you're wondering, yes, that is overweight. As the comedian in me might say, I wasn't overweight; I was just 8 inches too short.

What I didn't understand was that doing a lazy 45-minute lifting session four times a week wasn't going to offset the 3–4 nights of heavy drinking and 7 days of terrible diet. Trying to "work off" terrible eating habits is a recipe for disaster. I'm proof of that.

I realized that I had a lot in my life that was positive. I did! But if I couldn't control my alcohol intake, I would never be truly happy, so it was time for a change.

The key for me was taking that inventory and realizing there was a problem! I hadn't taken inventory of my life for years and years, so I got horrible results. Taking inventory of my life, my goals, my challenges, and where I was mentally, helped me realize there was a problem that needed fixed ASAP. Looking back, though, I wish I had told more people about my problem so I had some support.

In the summer of 2011, I decided to try something new to help me make a change. I had read some self-help articles that said writing in a journal could help me feel more fulfilled, so I thought that would be a great start. In addition, it would help me see how my life was going as I could look back on my writing and take inventory of where I stood on my path to success.

After journaling for a week or so, I learned that the best time for me to journal was when my feelings were most intense. Because I wanted to learn how to cut my alcohol intake, I thought I should journal on the mornings I woke up hungover. This happened to be most Fridays, Saturdays, and Sundays and sometimes Mondays.

I took the first 15 minutes of each hungover morning to think about what had happened the night before, and then I jotted down how I felt at that moment. The first morning I tried this, my journal entry read,

Oh my God. My head is pounding so bad right now. I feel like I don't want to do anything, and I'll probably just lie here a few more hours. I feel pathetic, and I think the only way to get myself back to not physically shaking is to have a couple shots. Wow my freaking head is killing me.

It was perfect that I started journaling only a few weeks before I met Chris Johnson, CEO of On Target Living, LLC, at a seminar I attended in the spring of 2011 where he talked about healthy living. This was a major, enlightening experience for me.

At one point, he spoke about how acidic and unhealthy some beverages are. "Even though diet soda doesn't have any calories," he said, "it can wreak havoc on our bodies and is very unhealthy for us." I remember exactly how I felt as I sipped a soda at that moment. I chuckled to myself and immediately lowered the drink to the floor, promising myself that I wouldn't take another sip. I went right up to Chris after his presentation.

He said, "It's great to meet you, Matt. What did you take away from what you heard today?"

I enthusiastically said, "Well Chris, as you talked about how awful diet soda is for our bodies and our cells, I looked at the one I was currently drinking and immediately put it down."

We both laughed. Then Chris said, "What are your goals with what you learned today?"

"I'm not sure yet," I responded, "but I do know I will be making some changes . I learned so much, and I took many notes."

We discussed healthy living for the next 30-45 minutes. I actually missed the next breakout session because he and I hit it off, and I was so energized by his knowledge and passion for being healthy.

Chris helped give me hope regarding my diet. I never fully understood how important diet was to looking and feeling healthy. I just thought if you worked out for hours every day that you could look as good as you wanted to. I never realized how important diet was to having more energy, a better physique, and fewer pimples on your face! That all sounded wonderful to me.

When he had to leave, I said, "I want to keep in touch with you and share my progress with you over time as I learn how to be healthier and start to conquer my body! I promise you'll be hearing from me, and I'm going to change my life!"

He smiled and said "I love your enthusiasm already and can tell you mean it. I'll definitely keep in touch with you as you start your journey."

I didn't realize at that time that the relationship with Chris would be my most important healthy living relationship that I had.

After that talk, I tried to use some of the ideas Chris described, and even went right to the grocery store after his presentation to stock up on all things healthy! I listened to Chris that summer and was inspired and excited that I had some new information I could use to potentially make some changes. I was enthusiastic about this new relationship and whole new outlook on what healthy really meant. But, the initial motivation and enthusiasm wore off due to my unwillingness to decrease my partying.

It would take more than Chris and his knowledge of healthy living to completely change my journey in life. It took me reaching a low point before I realized that change wasn't an option anymore; it was a necessity. It took until fall of 2011.

Halloween 2011

I love Halloween! Love it! I love dressing up and being able to be whoever I wanted for a night! It is a creative, fun, sexy night that everyone looks forward to each year. I always loved trying to come up with a fun or silly costume and taking pics of all the wild costumes everyone would wear.

But this Halloween was different. I partied hard like I did every Halloween weekend, but when I woke up the following morning, it happened. That post-Halloween-party Sunday morning would change the course of my life forever.

I woke up again on the floor of my living room. The TV was still on and at volume 75, so it was blasting music out of the speakers. It was 7 am, my head was throbbing, and the room was spinning. So I shut the TV off, and put my head back down on the rug so I could fall back asleep. But I couldn't. I was so hungover from the Halloween festivities the night before that I knew this was going to be one awfully long and painful Sunday. My stomach was churning, and I couldn't open my eyes because the sun was beaming into the room.

As I lifted my head off the floor, the strong smell of warm, skunked beer forced its way into my nostrils. The stench was so potent I had to tell myself to just breathe out of my mouth for a while, because if I didn't, the seven pieces of pizza I ate the night before were going to come back up.

As I forced my body off the ground and stood, I noticed the crushed beer cans that had surrounded me on the floor. The image startled me, but it also made sense. The cans looked like a chalk outline of me lying there. I was dead from alcohol. I was dead inside and didn't have a purpose anymore. I didn't have a burning drive, and I didn't have a reason to want to get out of bed before noon on the weekends. I had slowly killed myself with alcohol and unhealthy eating over the past decade.

I staggered to my futon in the living room as I sidestepped an empty pizza box and two half-eaten slices of pizza smashed into my rug from the previous night's festivities. The room was still spinning. I basically saw three futons in my dizzy state, but figured if I laid on the one in the middle, I would be ok. It took almost all my energy to walk 2 feet over there, and then my body became dead weight as I flopped onto the futon.

My eyes were still half open due to my increasingly painful hangover, but of course, I had to check my phone to see if anyone had texted me. Before I was able to check my texts, I hit the wrong button on my phone, and it was in selfie picture mode. The camera was pointed right on my face. "Eewwww, I don't want to see myself right now," I said. Quickly, I shut off the camera.

Then I thought about how I felt. I pulled my phone back out, turned it on selfie mode, and took a picture of my face.

I looked like I hadn't slept in weeks. My face was extremely pale. I didn't even have a neck anymore because of my weight gain, and I noticed how swollen my cheeks were. This face looked like someone who had no idea where he was going in his life. It was the perfect picture! It was the perfect way to remind me of how I felt most mornings.

I stared at the picture, wondering if I would still be waking up on my floor in my mid-30s. What about when I'm 45? Will I still be partying and unable to be social unless I've just slammed five or six shots of vodka? Will I ever be able to read in church without drinking a few shots beforehand? Will I still be overweight and unable to run up and down a basketball court without gasping for my breath in the next 5–10 years? If I stay stuck in this behavior for years down the road, I won't live long enough to enjoy life. I was slowly destroying my confidence, my appearance, and my liver all at once. Something needed to change.

I consider myself extremely lucky to have hit "rock bottom" at this point in my life, and I'm grateful that nothing worse happened. I could have been arrested, beat up, or who knows what else considering my level of drunkenness on the weekends. If I had continued the lifestyle I had fallen into, I can guarantee something extreme would have happened.

I pulled myself upright, slowly slumped off the futon and crawled upstairs so I could use the bathroom and attempt to wash my face with cold water, hoping that would make the hangover subside. As I made my way to the top of the steps, I could see into my bedroom, and I noticed my journal laying on my nightstand. It became a morning hangover routine for me to write in it, so I figured now wasn't the right time to break the routine. By the time I got to the top of the steps, my breathing was heavy, and my legs felt like I had just run a marathon.

My eyes were still half open as I plopped onto my bed and slowly reached for my journal. I opened it mistakenly to a page that had four or five entries, so I scanned them. That's when I noticed something: they were all very similar. Most of the passages had the same words and phrases, like "head is pounding," and "I feel awful and don't want to do anything," and "pathetic," and "I did it again." What was so eye-opening about that morning, though, was that I had never read any of the previous passages; I just kept writing and writing each and every morning after a night of drinking.

Taking inventory of my life led me to start journaling and journaling led me to my big realization. I clearly saw the **pattern** of what my life had become. This is why Halloween 2011 was different. I read journal entries that only spanned 4–5 months, but clearly, if I had been journaling for 10 years, the pattern would have been the same. It didn't take me long before I dropped my head down on my chest and completely broke down sobbing.

I cried because I felt as if I were just existing for the past decade. I wasn't actually *living* my life. Though I felt like I had been letting myself down, I was also crying happy tears, motivating tears, knowing this was the end of that part of my life. That day, I realized and started to mentally take ownership of why I had become who I was. Do you take ownership of your life? Think about that. Taking ownership of your life will help you understand that you have control of what you become in this world! And we are all capable of greatness! All of us!

Before this day, I blamed anything and anyone I could think of. I blamed my friends for "making me" drink with them. I blamed my circumstances because I lived in such a "party area"—it was obviously the bars' fault for making it so easy to drink in the Southside. I blamed the good Lord himself for not letting me be my true self while being sober.

Life will change once you take full ownership for all of your past decisions! The blame game was over, and it was time to own the decisions I made. I CHOSE to drink heavily, and my current situation was a result of that decision. But you know what else I could choose? I could make the decision to change my life. Starting that day!

That morning was the most emotional morning I had in my life up to that point. I continuously broke down crying, but that didn't stop me from reading and letting each word of every journal entry sink in. I wasn't punishing myself—I kept feeling more inspired to change as I sat there in my bed, with a huge hangover, reading all the entries about who I had become. I continued to read, and I continued to feel more motivated to never be that person again.

Benjamin Franklin once said, "Your net worth to the world is usually determined by what remains after your bad habits are subtracted from your good ones." I clearly had way too many bad habits in my life, and those habits needed to change.

The image of me lying on the floor with a beer can chalk outline of my body was the perfect symbol for this turning point in my life. Those bad habits needed to die right now. The man who slowly destroyed himself with alcohol over the last 10 years, was being buried right there on the floor that morning. He was gone. It was time for a different version of Matt Scoletti to emerge.

This was IT! This was the moment I needed to reach before I changed! Reading my journal entries over the past 5 months, and looking at my phone at that pathetic selfie I took were huge motivators. I could feel it already! I could feel that I had hit my breaking point!

Even though I was still painfully hungover, I had a new purpose, or should I say, "a" purpose. I let life shove me around for a decade, and now it was time to take back my life and turn it into the life I wanted to live. I knew I couldn't continue suffering this mental torture that I had subjected myself to for so long, and living a healthier lifestyle would be the motivation I could use to help me escape this self-created prison!

I had motivation, I was excited, and I jumped out of bed to begin living my new life! But something I also had . . . was a hangover still. I also found out that day that no amount of euphoria or motivation could kill a hangover. I had to laugh a bit at myself as I attempted to jump out of bed only to be smacked back down by those 10+ beers I drank the night before.

I decided on a more gentle approach to getting myself out of bed with the second attempt. This worked much better. The thunderous headache I had was slightly more bearable when moving slowly.

As I plodded to the bathroom to wash my face, I thought about some things that had happened recently in my life. I had just lost a close friend of mine because I was drinking heavily one night and said some awful things that I definitely shouldn't have. He called to say "hello" and see how I was doing on a Thursday night around 8 pm. I had been out for an hour by then and had done 5 shots before I left my house. He poked fun at me because I sounded tipsy, and I shot back that he wasn't worth my time and I didn't need friends like him in my life anymore. I only got mad at him because he was right. I also got mad at myself because alcohol was ruining some positive relationships that I had.

Then there was the famous late night call for pizza delivery every Friday and Saturday night. I would call the local pizza shop as I walked back to my house after a night of drinking, but I would never receive the pizza I ordered. The second I closed my door, I would pass out on the floor or on my futon in my living room.

The pizza guy would probably knock on the door a bunch of times, while I snored away in a drunken stupor. I bet after two or three times of this scenario, they would probably hang up after my call and say, "Hey guys, don't even bother taking a pizza to Scoletti's house. He won't answer the door. We can all just share his large cheese pizza between us." I started checking my bank account in the morning, and I always had a $9.95 charge from Genero's Pizza in the Southside because they would try to deliver my pizza, but nobody would answer.

Those stories and more circled around in my head as I washed my face. Stories from having a few drinks before going in to work some mornings when I was in Boston, to being so drunk at a church function in the Southside that they asked me to leave before I really embarrassed myself.

Instead of beating myself up over these stories, I told myself the true story. I was still the same person who got voted into homecoming court and was the most outgoing, personable guy I knew just 10 years prior. It was inside of me! I just had to find it! I couldn't go on living my life knowing I wasn't living anywhere close to my potential. Life had taken me by the throat, eaten me alive, chewed me up, and spit me back out. I ALLOWED life take over, and I lost control of who I was, my values, and my goals and dreams.

Growing up, I valued God, family, my friends, my attitude, and basketball. Now, I still valued God and family first, which was great. However, my other values became drinking alcohol, partying, and befriending others who went down that same path. This had to stop, and I had to shift my values if I wanted to succeed.

I washed my face that morning and thought, "A decade of living like this is enough!" Could I have learned my lesson 3 years ago? 5 years ago? 7 years ago? Maybe. But I couldn't dwell on the "what ifs." I had plenty of life to live, and that living needed to start NOW!

My excitement continued to increase as I could truly feel this was going to be a monumental day, one that I would put on my calendar for years to come. How did I know for sure? Because I had long passed the thought of, "Oh wow, I need to slow down my drinking." I was at the point where I made a decision that I wouldn't allow alcohol to run my life. I would start to carve out the life I wanted to create...on my terms!

I walked back downstairs with a little more bounce in my step after my epiphany and after washing my face. I went into the living room and began picking up empty beer cans, and as I did, for the first time in almost a decade, I felt a little bit of hope.

I reminisced about when I graduated from high school at 5'8" and 165 pounds. I had a blazing quick first step on the basketball court and was the fastest guy on our team running sprints during practice. Now, as I stood in my living room cleaning up the slices of pizza, I was 5'8" and 215 pounds. I had put on 50 pounds in 10 years. 50 pounds! I was now a 27-year-old guy, 6 years out from college, and I couldn't even play basketball for very long without getting completely winded and worn out. I remember one of my buddies saying "That's ok, we are getting older, and this is what happens." Older? I was 27, not 80. That thought helped fuel my cause for change.

I thought about my weight gain as I threw out the pizza, and then I thought about the changes I could potentially make. I went to the kitchen to grab a water and saw the Food Target on my fridge, which basically showed healthy foods in green and went through yellow and orange to foods you should stay away from in red. Chris Johnson had handed it out during his presentation. I wasn't surprised that the majority of my diet showed up in the red area. Ok, I need to get rid of the foods that are in the red and orange then. I began emptying the fridge of leftover Chinese food, other processed foods, beers, and trans fat-laced items.

As I dumped the beers into the sink, I had one of the most empowering feelings I ever had. I watched as each beer drained and told myself that alcohol would no longer control who I was, and it certainly wasn't going to sabotage my goals and dreams anymore!

As the beer poured out, I thought about how all of my actions led me to this point. Alcohol began as a fun social lubricant in college and slowly turned into a necessity for me to be social later in my life. That is a scary transition as booze went from a want to a need.

If you are getting ready to go to college, I don't want you to make the same mistake that I did. I beg you to have fun, be social, and make friends. But keep your drinking under control or you'll end up exactly how I did, or worse.

Another beer flowed down my kitchen sink drain, and I could feel more enthusiasm burning inside me. I had no idea where I was going with this not drinking idea—or how I would accomplish it—but as I felt the beer can get lighter from the contents spilling out, the smile on my face became bigger and bigger. I felt so alive!

As the last beer from the fridge spilled out, I looked outside at my back patio to see the destruction there from the night before. My small row house in the Southside of Pittsburgh had a 20' by 20' slab of concrete as a patio and then a 30' by 20' grass back yard. As I stepped outside, I felt the cool air of a beautiful fall morning, and my face was struck by the beating sun as it shined down upon the entire back yard. This was when I felt my hangover kick into high gear. But I didn't worry about that because I was becoming a new person that day. The back patio was covered in empty beer cans, some still half full from the night before. Dozens of red Solo cups were lying all over the ground and under my folding table from beer pong. Four ping pong balls rolled around as the wind blew them back and forth on the concrete. I began to clean up the mess.

Two large garbage bags later, my back yard was clean. I left the garbage bags out back and took a seat on a chair outside while chugging a water. I remember how gorgeous the morning was. It was almost heavenly that morning as the cool breeze wisped across my face. I relaxed in my folding chair, starring up at the clouds rolling by in the bright blue sky. Then my mind began to wander again. A lot of nights I would walk home and barely even remember the walk when I woke up the next morning. The nights I do remember walking home, I often thought about how I'd feel if I were in great shape and wasn't embarrassed to take my shirt off (and suck in my beer gut) at the pool anymore. I would start playing the Rocky soundtrack in my head as I stumbled home drunkenly.

After a while, I walked back inside to grab another water to help hydrate myself. Again, on the fridge, I noticed Chris Johnson's food target. I had already thrown out the majority of my food because it was in the "bad" food section of the food target, so I set off to the grocery store to buy food in the green or healthier food section.

My head still throbbed as I pulled into the grocery store parking lot around 1pm that Sunday. I loaded my cart with eggs, egg whites, Greek yogurt, leafy greens, almond milk, oats, fruit, chicken, mineral water, and some other healthy options.

The cashier said, "Wow! Somebody is a healthy boy today." I guess I had been in her line before, and my cart looked different in the past. I chuckled to myself and thought, "I'm not going to be a healthy boy just today. I want to be a health guy for good now!" I smiled at her and said, "Yes, it's time to make a few changes." She smiled back. "Good for you, honey. Have a great Sunday!"

My drive home was only about 5 minutes since the store was close. But it was a glorious 5 minutes! It was an even more amazing 10 minutes unloading the car and seeing how different my refrigerator looked when it was full of healthy food. One of the keys to healthy living that I learned through this process was that if I only had healthy food in the house, that is all I would eat. I knew I was too lazy to drive out and buy unhealthy food when I could easily just eat the healthy stuff in my house.

After all the food was unloaded, I made some scrambled eggs with three whole eggs and three egg whites and cut up an apple as I sat in my living room and ate. Within 2 minutes, my phone buzzed, and a text came through from a friend I had been out with the night before. The text read: "What time we heading over to the BBQ?" I smiled to myself because it didn't take long before the bad decisions could easily take over. Normally, we would head over to my friend's house around 4 pm and have beers all day on Sunday Funday.

Not this Sunday. I responded, "Sorry man, I have some other stuff I need to take care of. You have fun though."

He said, "What are you talking about? I'll swing by around 3:30."

Again, I pushed back. "Sorry, I won't even be here. Going to have dinner with my family."

I wasn't really seeing my family that day, but I had plans to start getting my mind in the right place that afternoon. I'm not proud that I lied to my friend, but this lifestyle change was so new that I wasn't sure how else to handle it.

When I was a teenager, if something went wrong, or I just needed to let off some steam, I'd go into my parent's basement, turn on some loud music, and workout. Even if it was 10 pm, I'd still do it. It felt so good to hit a punching bag, jump rope, shadow box, lift some weights, dance around the room, and just get into a zone where all of my worries were gone. After telling my buddy I wasn't going to the BBQ, I felt like going back to my teenager days. I had a punching bag and some weights in the basement of my current house, as well as one of the most badass speaker systems on the planet.

I changed into some workout attire around 5 pm, brought a couple waters with me to the basement, put on the *Rocky* soundtrack, and worked out. I let out a lot of bottled up energy and frustration with myself on the punching bag. I also had a mirror down there to shadow box in front of—basically just throwing punches at the air in different sequences. It's a great workout. I kept saying, "C'mon Matt! Keep at it. You got this! Keep punching and punching and punching! You are getting healthier!"

I kept punching until I was extremely tired and drank both of my bottles of water. I thought, "Wow! What a workout! I'm soaking wet! I feel great, even though I struggled through some of this, but I'm happy I came down here. I must have been down here at least an hour by now." I walked upstairs and saw that it was only 5:15 pm. I had only been downstairs for 15 minutes working out. I was shocked.

My cardiovascular strength was low, and my heart was racing after only 15 minutes of punching the heavy bag and doing some pushups. I gave myself a pep talk. "That's ok Matt, this is just the start." I walked back downstairs and slowly paced around, throwing a punch or two every time I approached the heavy bag. I thought about the alternative to what I was doing that night. "I could be on my fifth beer right now, laughing and hanging out with friends . . . as I drove myself further into serious alcoholism." Nope, I'm happy right here, right now, and I'm happy to be sweating and feeling halfway decent about getting in a work out.

I took a shower, drank more water, and sat down in front of a bowl of Greek yogurt with fruit and oats in it. I actually enjoyed this snack because it packed a huge protein punch, and was a healthy option. Also, it was the easiest thing to make—only 60 seconds from start to finish.

I had been working on healthy eating slowly for months before that day, so I was already used to the flavor and texture of Greek yogurt. It had become something I enjoyed for a snack or meal. After meeting Chris Johnson over the summer, I was a relatively healthy eater from Monday through Thursday.

It took me a while to get used to the taste of Greek yogurt, almond milk, flaxseeds, organic peanut butter, and Ezekiel bread. But after implementing a couple of these healthy foods at a time—and not trying to change everything all at once like I did the first time—eating healthier became easier. I used a Confucius quote to help keep me motivated: "It does not matter how slowly you go, so long as you do not stop." I knew making slow, small changes would be the best way to adjust to this new lifestyle.

A lot of the foods Chris wanted me to try were tasty, so I started researching foods that were an upgrade from what I was currently consuming. I learned that healthy eating doesn't mean everything has to taste horrible. Our society tries to persuade us that healthy foods are boring foods, but that myth couldn't be further from the truth.

I finally started to wrap my brain around the fact that by eating these new, healthier foods, I would be treating my body the way it should be treated. It was a small step into the world of becoming healthier, feeling more energized, and getting back the life and body I had lost years before. I was hoping that my healthier eating would also help with my confidence, but I had to complement that with reducing my alcohol intake to see real change.

If you decide to change your eating habits, please be patient. I'm a certified health coach, and I've never seen anyone succeed in the "lose a ton of weight in a short amount of time" eating plan where you basically starve yourself for 30–90 days to lose a ton of weight. That's because your body then rebels against you because you've deprived it of calories for so long, so you'll eventually overeat and gain back all the weight you lost. In most cases, you'll weigh more by the end of the cycle than you did when you began the diet. Don't fall into this trap.

My body rewarded me for healthier eating 3.5 days a week, but my alcohol abuse and overeating on Thursday to Sunday was enough to keep me from making any real progress. I hoped that would change when I hit my breaking point.

As I sat on my futon in the living room after I ate my Greek yogurt that day, I thought, "Ok, what now?" It was only 7 pm. Normally, I would be out socializing at this time, but I didn't have anywhere to be since I dumped plans with my friends.

I pulled out my phone and read texts from three of the people I knew would be at the BBQ that night. Then I deleted the conversations instead of pondering if I should reach out to them and stop over. I couldn't. I made a new promise to myself. It was time for a change.

I decided to go to bed early that pleasant night, the day after Halloween, almost because I didn't know what else to do. It was 9:00 pm. It was the earliest I had gone to bed on a weekend in 10 years without being blackout drunk.

I didn't fall asleep right away though. I reread some of my journal entries from the previous months. Again, I shed a few tears. These tears were different though. These tears were joyful because I did something that I hadn't done in almost a decade that Sunday: I didn't have *one* alcoholic beverage, and I worked out. Wow. Why was *this* such a huge step for me? Because before that day, I didn't even think that was possible for me to do. Think about that. I didn't think it was possible for me not to drink on a weekend day, plus complete a workout. That is a sad mental state to be in. But, that day, I felt different as I lay in my bed. I knew it. It was the start of something totally different. I wasn't quite sure what the plan was, but I took a step in the right direction that day! Around 10 pm, I thought "Good night, Matt. Congratulations on one small victory today."

*****

The next morning was euphoric and also funny. I woke up to my alarm at 7:20 am. I gave the same Monday morning "uugghhhhhh . . . my head is—" but then, "Wait a second...my head does NOT hurt." I was fully prepared to give myself the hopeless, pointless "I'm never drinking again" pep talk, but it wasn't necessary because I didn't drink the night before! I also woke up to the first alarm! I actually laughed. I had an extra 45 minutes on my hands. Should I go back to bed? No way! I just slept for 8.5+ hours, and I felt great!

I looked over at my nightstand at my journal. I smiled. I was about to write my first positive journal entry ever. What a milestone! It read: "I woke up this Monday morning to my FIRST alarm! WHAT?!? I'm shocked with myself! Yesterday was the first Sunday in years that I didn't have a drink . . . AND I worked out! Yes, this is Matt Scoletti and this is my journal. Nobody stole my journal, this is me! I'm happy, I feel great, and this is an exciting step in my life!" That was a new type of journal entry that I could get used to.

A Monday morning felt beautiful for the first time in years! I jumped out of bed and gave thanks for being alive today and having a second chance at life! As my feet hit the floor, I looked up and said, "Yes! I get to play again!" And it felt like the first day of a long, fun journey that I was about to embark on.

The other healthy living concept I learned to do first thing in the morning was to drink a glass of water. After sleeping for 7–9 hours, our bodies are slightly dehydrated because they've gone a long time without water. So I figured along with jumping out of bed and being thankful to be alive, I'd drink a glass of water, throw some cold water on my face, and have a healthy snack.

After my small victories of waking up on time, feeling refreshed from not being hungover, and seeing the beauty the morning had to offer, I learned the value of waking up energized! I knew this had to be the way I woke up each morning if I truly wanted to change my life. This rejuvenated uplifted version of myself this early in the morning needed to happen with regularity. I made a pact with myself that day that I'd wake up quickly each morning and say thanks for being alive as soon as I got up.

That Monday morning, I seriously think my car levitated to work! I swear I was skipping through the front door of the office building, and I felt a new life inside of me that I could have never dreamed of! And I hadn't really done much at all . . . yet! One day of not drinking combined with one workout? That was it! I couldn't help but think, "If I feel THIS good after only one day without drinking, imagine how good

I'll feel after the next month!" I was unstoppable now, and I craved more and more sobriety and energy!

When I hit my breaking point, I will admit, that didn't mean everything changed right away and I became a new person. Oh no, not after 10 years of doing the same thing over and over again. I couldn't reverse that in a day. I tried to tell myself that, but I also knew this could be a starting point for change. Have *you* ever had a breaking point? That point in your life, no matter if it's with work, a relationship, your weight, or anything else, where you said, "THAT'S IT! I've had ENOUGH!" And you decide it's time to change? It was one of the most empowering feelings I ever had.

I often wonder why it took so long for me to make positive changes in my life. I think I know why I didn't change though, and also why a lot of other people don't make changes. In my head, I told myself the story that the pain of changing would be much worse than the pain of staying right where I was. The only time you truly change is when you learn to link more pain to staying the same than you do to changing. If we think it'll be less painful to change, we are much more likely to make that change.

Let's use an example of someone who is trying to quit smoking. Why do they keep smoking? Because it makes them feel good, and they link pleasure to smoking, right? If they quit smoking for a while, sometimes it's painful for them to stop, and they constantly think about that next cigarette.

What if every time that person THOUGHT about a cigarette, they pulled out a picture of what lungs look like after years of smoking? That same person could visit a hospital once a week and see patients that suffered from emphysema due to smoking. Then, in their minds, they begin to link pain to continuing to smoke. Once they link more pain to continuing to smoke than to quitting the habit, it becomes easier to quit.

I use this example because it directly relates to the problem I had. It was so easy to live my life the same way I had for years, but when I linked that ugly selfie I took and those painful journal entries to staying the same, I knew it would be much easier and more beneficial to make a healthy change.

The same "linking" idea can be used with someone who doesn't want to work out. Most of the time they link working out to something negative like feeling tired and run down. But they could use their love of a specific musical artist to their advantage. If they only played music from that artist while they were working out, then that person could eventually enjoy working out because they would start to link that fun music to being able to exercise. You can give this a try with anything you are trying to change in your life!

I consider myself very lucky because the timing of my journaling for a few months, then meeting Chris, and then reaching my breaking point that day couldn't have happened any better. I felt the potential for a sense of purpose, even though all I knew was that I wanted to start getting healthier and in better shape.

Journaling saved my life, and my journaling always occurred within 15 minutes of me waking up in the morning. As I wrote in my journal each morning and reflected on my life—how things have been and how I want them to change—I learned a lot about myself. I learned that if I could figure out a way to continue making journaling and starting my day right top priorities, then I could slowly make some progress to become the person I knew was inside me. Even if I only had the first 10 or 15 minutes of my morning structured, I felt like that could make a huge impact not only on that day, but on my life. It turns out, I was right.

This was a completely new concept for me, and journaling helped birth the First 15 model without me even knowing it. Little did I know that toward the end of 2011, I would have stumbled upon a concept that would eventually lead to a complete turnaround in my life. This was a crucial period when I figured out if I could completely control the start to my day, it could help propel me to an even better morning, day, week, year, and LIFE!

*****

Current First 15:

5 minutes—WAKE UP! (after 7–9 hours of sleep). Stretch, water, water, snack.

How to do it: Stand with feet on the floor, get excited, and say "YES! I get to play again!" Put your hands up in the air as you say this. Touch your toes and hold for a few seconds to stretch out the body. Then drink 8–12 oz. of water, throw ice cold water on your face, and have a healthy snack.

5 minutes—Write in journal.

5 minutes—Check social media, watch TV, fumble around on my phone.

Analysis: A huge milestone was met by not waking up hungover! It was also great to be thankful for waking up again and being able to play again in this world. Drinking water first thing in the morning helped my body stay hydrated. Throwing water on my face this early in the morning helped me fully wake up and forced me to do something that I didn't necessarily want to do. It is a great discipline. Having a healthy snack and/or breakfast in the morning is a great way to tell your body, "It's time to get up and live!" I still journaled in the morning and enjoyed doing that, but other than waking up and journaling, my mornings were mainly TV watching, checking my phone, and wasting time before it was time to head to work. I knew I could still make a lot of improvements.

Chapter 4 – Your Self-Talk is Paramount to Your Success

"Relentless, repetitive self-talk is what changes our self-image."

~ Denis Waitley

You didn't think I actually succeeded in not drinking and everything went perfect and smooth after that Sunday afternoon did you? Ok good, because that's not how it went.

As I started my journey to healthy living, I knew I had my On Target Living buddy, Chris Johnson, on my side. After hearing Chris speak the first time, I attempted to change about 50 things at once with my diet, but when I noticed I couldn't change every single thing about my diet all at once, I said, "Forget this healthy crap," and I went back to my old ways of fried food, trans-fat heaven, and eating whatever I wanted during weekends of binge drinking. I learned that it was better to slowly upgrade my food and not drive myself insane trying to change 10 years of unhealthy eating in two days.

Chris and I shared a few emails and a phone call over the next few days after my initial exciting Monday morning. He helped me with upgrading my peanut butter to organic peanut butter, and we figured out that eating 5–7 small meals a day might work better than the normal three large (and sometimes way too large) meals a day I was currently eating. He told me to slowly implement these ideas into my lifestyle instead of trying to change everything all at once. And I couldn't agree more with him, especially after my repeated failures with trying to change a lot of things very quickly.

This made sense because diets typically don't last. And this wasn't a diet I was trying for a few months. I wanted to make a lifestyle change! Rather, I didn't WANT to make a lifestyle change; I WAS making a lifestyle change. I didn't give myself the option of backing out. I was 100% full-on committed to this.

Chris and I began to form this bond that I hoped would last a long time. But many of my other relationships weren't as excited about my new lifestyle. Have you ever heard the Jim Rohn quote, "You are the average of the five people you spend the most time with?" I believe it is true because that is exactly what I had become. The four guys I hung out with the most would start drinking every Thursday around 7 pm and wouldn't stop pounding beers until late Sunday night. It made sense because I liked drinking and partying, as well.

If I wrote down who my best friends were at that point in my life, those four guys would have been in my top five. The first few weeks of my lifestyle change were extremely difficult because I was finally doing something that made me feel good, but my best friends were all calling me a "wuss" and telling me to quit being a hermit and come out with them.

I want to mention something at this point. I'm not blaming my friends. It was *my* decision to get drunk, and they didn't force-feed me drinks. Guy friends typically poke fun at each other and laugh with each other. I'm no angel either, and I've been an enabler many times in my life, telling friends or family members to do a shot with me or saying, "Don't be a pansy, it's only a fun night out." These four guys were decent people, and I actually still keep in touch with one of them today. But we all shared one bad habit, which was leading me down a path that I no longer wanted.

For the first few weeks, I didn't go out with them at all. I couldn't. I didn't trust myself to be around my best friends because I was too scared I'd end up drunk. It was too early in my transition to take that step yet. I needed more time. That didn't stop them from calling and texting me consistently, though, trying to lure me back to the bar scene. I started using the excuse that I couldn't be out late because I knew I'd never get up in the morning to work out. That excuse worked for a little while, but they kept on me.

So, I decided to take it to the next level. I asked the owner of my local gym if I could work for one hour in the morning and open up the gym. Our gym opened at 6 am on Monday–Friday and 7 am on Saturday and Sunday. I begged him to let me work from 6–7 am on Monday–Friday and 7–8 am on Saturday and Sunday.

He laughed. "Of course you can. The guy who opens the gym prefers to sleep in another hour anyway."

Now I was obligated to be at the gym in the morning because I was an employee of the gym. This was awesome! My friends didn't think this was so awesome.

I received texts like "What are you doing man? You took a job in the morning at the gym? You're an idiot, dude. Peace out." And "You are joking right? Who works at 6 am on a Friday? Get your priorities straight man. You are in your mid-20s." I believe I WAS finally starting to get my priorities straight.

Something interesting happened as my friends continued to come down on me, though. I started to care less and less about what they thought of my new attitude and outlook on life, though it isn't easy when your core friend base continues to make fun of you and question your lifestyle. But I felt like I was finally making progress in my life, and I wasn't going back to the old me.

Maybe I'm just stubborn. Or maybe I knew I needed to change or my life would not turn out how I wanted it to. I learned a key rule to live life on my terms throughout this process: What other people think of me is NONE of my business. That rule helped me create the body and life that I wanted and needed to feel happy and fulfilled!

If you are thinking about making a healthy change in your life, that doesn't necessarily mean you'll lose friends over it. It's possible that your friends will support you right away. I didn't have that experience until I upgraded my friends to a healthier group, but I hope, if you decide to change, that your friends will have your back no matter what.

I had a difficult time explaining to mine the severity of what I was going through. I could have taken each of them aside to let them in on the secret that I was an alcoholic, and I could have asked them for support. Had I done this, who knows, maybe I could have inspired our whole group to change together.

I could have turned my "naysayer" friends into my biggest supporters! I challenge you to have those tough conversations with friends about a change you are trying to make; it could be a stepping stone that leads to an even stronger relationship. You'll never know until you give it a shot.

If you are trying to make a change in your life, it makes sense to tell a few of your close friends and family members. Then gage how they react to your proposed changes or struggles. That will give you a good indicator if they will be supporters of your journey—whether your goal is to be healthier, wealthier, stronger, smarter, or anything in between—or someone who will hold you back and keep you stuck.

Only align yourself with people who will support you and help you move toward your goals. Life is too short to spend time with people who try to bring you down to their level. Rather, step up a level and surround yourself with pleasant, uplifting, organized, enthusiastic people. Then, you will become more like them!

I challenge you to look in your phone and see who the last five people are that you've texted with. Or, for you non-texters (I know there are still some of you out there . . . ahem . . . my father), think about the last 3-5 phone conversations you've had. In both situations think about the conversations and how you normally feel during and afterward. Is this someone who supports you? Is this person a positive influence on your life? Are *you* a positive influence on their life? Do you feel better or worse after the conversation?

My challenge is NOT to remove a friend from your life. My challenge is for you to start noticing who's in your life and how each person makes you feel. This way, you'll learn to harness and cherish the close friends that you do have, and possibly fade away from the ones who make you feel negative. Please accept the challenge! It'll change your life!

Depending on your relationship with your family, talk to your siblings, parents, and/or other family members about your struggle. I was too scared to see the reactions of my parents and brother, so I never reached out to them. I'm sure with their support my battle wouldn't have felt so lonely, and I probably would have grown closer to my family because of their part in my successful journey back to sobriety. Please don't make my mistake! Open up and share your struggle with those close to you!

A close friend of mine, John, was struggling with alcohol and was overweight. I coached John, and we came to the conclusion that he needed to tell his family about his alcohol problem. After he revealed his problem, John called me and said, "Matt, after getting all of that off my chest, I feel so incredible. Some of my family was shocked, but they all supported my decision to get myself away from drinking. I'm not saying this will be easy, but knowing I have their support makes things so much better for me."

If your family isn't supportive at all, confide in a close friend or professional to get the help you need. Getting professional help would have been another smart route for me to take, but I never did. I could have saved myself from years of suffering working with a professional.

I thought that because I got myself into this situation by myself, I should be able to get myself out of it by myself. I didn't hit rock bottom because of something that I couldn't control. I took all of those drinks myself, so I was determined to fix it myself.

Plus, I couldn't just tell someone that I thought I might be an alcoholic, could I? I wasn't even sure I was one. I don't drink early in the morning, so I don't need help, right? I was also afraid of being "labeled" an alcoholic if I sought help. The stigma of having an addiction can be a worse problem than the actual substance being used. That is how society can sometimes make it feel anyway. That is why I think talking to friends, family, or professionals about our problems and addictions would increase people's chances of overcoming that addiction. It can be so difficult to do that at the time. But it is necessary.

*****

My journey continued, and the nutrition part of the lifestyle change was a wild and unique ride. Since my breakdown and breakthrough on the day after Halloween, November 2011 was incredible. I kept in constant contact with Chris Johnson, and I asked him many questions about nutrition, diet, eating habits, and lifestyle changes. He was a huge supporter of me changing a lot of things about my life and had my back through it all. He went through similar struggles as I did decades before me, so he knew the ropes and how to help me meet my goals.

Outside of the discussions between Chris and I was this thing called "the real world" and society. We all know how society is with food in the United States. You drive down a main road in the USA and you'll see fast food place after fast food place. That means foods that are normally loaded with sodium and trans fats—overall the most unhealthy foods on earth. But that is the norm.

If I got on the elevator at my office holding a big bag of fast food, people would say, "Oh boy, what floor are you getting off on, I might have to join you for lunch!" But, after I started bringing in homemade chicken, lentils, leafy greens, and quinoa in large bags or Tupperware, I got very different looks on the elevator. One morning on the elevator, a woman saw my bags of Tupperware containers full of healthy food and gave me a look like, "Are you serious?" It can feel weird here in the United States to eat very healthy. But guess what? I prefer weird and healthy to conforming and being unhealthy any day of the year!

Society had pushed me around for a long time and that's what will happen to you if you aren't careful. If you don't have a plan, or goals, or a vision for yourself, this world will force you to your knees and create a life for you. I can speak from experience. When I graduated college, my only goal was to get a job. Once I got a job, my only goal was to keep that job. I didn't have a purpose and didn't have any idea the direction I wanted my life to go. So I went the direction that society pushed me. That is a recipe for a life that you won't be proud of and a legacy that will be meaningless.

Choose your destiny! It is your life, your dream, and your choice to live life on your terms! Know what you are passionate about, make plans, and do everything in your power to achieve that dream. Will setbacks occur? Yes! Will it be easy? No! Will you want to quit sometimes? Probably. Will it be worth it in the end? Absolutely!

Where we are today is a direct result of the decisions we made in the past. That is a fact. As soon as I owned the fact that I was overweight and a functional alcoholic because that was the result of my own decisions, it helped me completely change my life. I owned my faults. Now it was time to own my future!

I valued my health, my future, and my purpose, so I didn't mind the stares when I walked into the elevator on Monday morning with giant bags of grilled chicken, protein powder, green beans, and brown rice. Society could stare at me all day . . . in fact, they would be staring at me not long after this . . . but more on that later.

If you make a decision to get healthier, it's naïve to assume it's going to be all sunshine and rainbows. You'll have to make some tough decisions for sure. Change doesn't come easy. Obstacles will constantly be in your way on your journey to a healthier you. You may be out with your friends at happy hour, and someone buys a round of shots. Or you could be at work, and someone brings in cookies that you have to walk by every time you are going to the bathroom. If you make a stand, you'll have to have the guts to stand up for yourself.

What you need to be careful of is to not just eat crappy food out of boredom or convenience. In the office cookie example, a lot of employees will eat the cookies because they are there. Not because they are hungry. My wife and I will indulge in some frozen yogurt or sweets every now and then, but we do not make a habit of eating junk food. That way, it's almost like a celebration when we actually do, and it makes the experience more memorable.

The healthier I became throughout my process, the less I craved unhealthy foods. Not once since my lifestyle change have I said, "Oh man, I could really go for those loaded bacon and cheese French fries." I know what they will do to my body and how I'll feel afterwards, so it isn't worth it to me. I'm not suggesting my method is the right one for you, but I figured if I felt amazing, younger, stronger, and more energized when eating healthy, why would I want junk food anymore? I know some people use the 80/20 rule where 80% of the time you eat healthy, and 20% you eat what you want. I support that rule if it works for your style, but it just wasn't my best option for me.

It sounds simple when someone says, "Just stop eating unhealthy foods," during these times of temptation. That's a great idea, until you are at a restaurant and everyone orders burgers and onion rings or chicken strips and fries or a huge plate of spaghetti. When it's your turn to tell the server your order, the pressure builds, and sometimes it feels like you are standing on a Broadway stage with the lights shining right in your face. *What are you going to order for dinner?*

Sometimes peer pressure can break you, and you'll order an unhealthy meal like everyone else (even though you don't want to). But sometimes, that's your chance to shine and order that grilled fish with veggies and quinoa. The question is, "What decision will you make?" Will you have the self-discipline to do it?

Self-discipline is something I learned about so much throughout my body and mind transformation. I had no self-discipline for so many years. The amazing thing is many people know what is best for them but they still don't do it. People know they should stop smoking, start working out, or drink less, but they never change. We consistently do things to our minds and bodies that we KNOW are bad for us because we don't have the self-discipline to make a change. But you aren't just anybody! You will create the life you want and have the self-discipline to make your biggest goals happen!

If your reason for changing is deep enough and your values are strong enough, then you can achieve any outcome that you want. If your "why" is strong enough, then you can deal with any situation that may present itself. When society gets really tough for you, think about the deep reason you wanted to change, hold onto that reason and you WILL be strong enough to push through.

You only get one chance at this crazy thing we call "life." And what I realized after 10 years of just existing was it was time for me to live my life and take full ownership of it—full ownership by becoming sober, full ownership with my workouts and getting stronger, and full ownership regarding my nutrition, which many would say is the toughest part.

*****

Since the first day of my lifestyle change, I had been keeping my promise of getting healthier each and every day. After three weeks of my healthy living journey, I still hadn't had a drink! It was a huge breakthrough for me! This was the first time in over a decade that I'd gone three whole weeks without a single sip of alcohol.

Remember when I used to hit the snooze five times before waking up? Not anymore! Now, I set my alarm for 5:40 am, and I was up and ready to go as soon as the alarm went off! Why? Because I had a purpose now! I had a healthy living purpose, and I made a promise to myself to get healthier. Also, my bedtime moved back from around 11:30 pm to around 10 pm.

"BEEP BEEP BEEP BEEP BEEP!" I woke up on the third Monday of my sobriety with another huge smile on my face! My feet hit the floor in my bedroom; I reached up in the air and said, "Yes! I get to play again!" Then I stretched for a few seconds, threw some water on my face, and wrote in my journal just to tell myself how good I was feeling. Then, I went to the kitchen to eat a banana and drink 8 oz. of water to get my body ready for a workout. Then, I sat on the floor in my living room and just thought about how far I had come in the last three weeks. I gave thanks to God for helping me stay strong during this lifestyle change. I put on my headphones as I walked four blocks to the gym and got myself pumped up for my one-hour workout before work. As I walked that Monday morning, I thought about the change in my mornings between that day, and four weeks ago.

After smacking the snooze button several times, my first 15 minutes in the morning used to consist of me scrambling around my house getting clothes ready, showering, shaving (and normally cutting myself 2–3 times), and then scarfing down a pop tart or some other unhealthy snack before weaving in and out of traffic to make it to work by 9 am. Three weeks later as I walked into work, I had already woken up without snoozing the alarm, didn't have a hangover, worked out, prayed, wrote in my journal, showered/shaved, and ate a healthy breakfast. What progress! I was addicted to my new lifestyle already and didn't want to look back.

Mornings went from hell to heaven in a matter of three weeks! Yes, this *was* a fast transition and not everyone's morning will become that amazing in 3 weeks. But for me, it was a change I had been trying to make for years, so when it finally started to become a habit, I was immediately excited about it. This wasn't because my body was changing yet, even though I had lost a couple pounds.

I was in heaven in the morning because my mindset was changing: I was changing the story I told myself about who I was. I had a purpose and a vision to become the healthiest version of myself that I could become. It was absolutely incredible and the best feeling. I started to realize how important those first 15 minutes were in the morning. I thought if I could get the first 15 minutes of my day right, then that would trickle down to the rest of my day and help me have more energy, stay more focused, and be able to live a healthier, more fun, and happier life!

I understand some people may never be able to wake up at 5 or 6 am and work out or be extremely productive at that hour, and that's ok. You absolutely do not have to be a "morning person" to benefit from this book. I strongly suggest waking up 5–15 minutes earlier than normal and getting into the habit of a morning routine though. If this routine will give you more energy and help you live a more productive and happy life, then how can you afford to *not* wake up a few minutes earlier?

As my healthy living journey progressed, my morning routine and my lifestyle change were becoming a habit. I had made enough poor decisions on my own. This was when I began to learn about how my self-talk was affecting my life. The things I said to myself before, such as not being able to be fun when sober, just weren't true. I began to understand that my "pep talks" to myself and what I thought about myself would eventually become reality.

As I learned more about self-talk, I realized I needed to make this a part of my morning routine. My self-talk had drastically changed over the last three weeks, and that helped me understand that I could create the life I wanted and not cling to my old ways. **I figured if I could give myself a pep talk every morning about the person I wanted to become, then eventually, I would become that person.** This was one of the most life-changing concepts ever!

Every morning, after I'd wake up, I began saying to myself, "I am getting healthier! I love the changes I'm making! I control my own destiny, and there is no going back! I got this! I'm unstoppable!" Sometimes my energized talk to myself would be the Ayn Rand quote, "The question isn't 'Who is going to let me?' It's 'Who is going to stop me?'" These two pep talks became my mantras for months. I would make minor changes to them based on how I felt that day or if I was going after a specific goal, but these were my main pep talks each morning. And guess what? When you say something with a ton of emotion, and with sincere intensity 10+ times each morning, you begin to believe it! It was such a unique and awesome addition to my morning routine that I still do it each morning after waking up.

Looking back, another part of my issue between high school and my alcoholic days was love. I used to love life, love others, and also love who I was. Then I fell out of love with myself for almost a decade and lost my identity. If I couldn't love myself first, it affected everything else around me.

I believe loving one's self isn't selfish but rather necessary to be able to live the life you desire and to reach your potential. Once I started loving who I was again, I was able to show so much more love toward family, new friends, and even complete strangers. Love is what ultimately helped me kill the alcoholic demon inside me. My pep talks helped me love myself again and realize that I was a badass and could reach my goals! The pep talk is a skill that you need to learn and master. Positive self-talk will change your life!

Even if you are trying to lose weight or don't feel great physically, love who you are. You have so much to give to this world, no matter if you are 100 pounds or 400 pounds. You don't have to lose weight to love yourself. Love yourself now! Love who you are, but always look for ways to improve. That's what the pep talk will help you accomplish! Then, love yourself even more as you improve on yourself and love the healthy living journey you are on. Keep your positive self-talk a must every day of your life.

Adding a pep talk to my morning routine was wonderful. It helped make the rest of the day much more productive, and I felt so much more confident in myself. I could tell that it was already beginning to work.

*****

Current First 15:

5 minutes—WAKE UP! "Yes, I get to play again!" Stretch, water, water, snack.

2 minutes—Pep Talk. I began to learn the importance of my self-talk. I learned that my confidence level could change based on how I perceived myself, and with a strong pep talk each morning, I could basically become whoever I wanted to be.

The First 15

<u>How to do it:</u> Stand in front of the mirror. Pick a strong pep talk and repeat it ten times each morning! You can switch up your pep talk as needed, but say it with STRONG conviction and tone! "I am larger than life!" "I am unstoppable!" This is KEY: the pep talk is in PRESENT TENSE! Not "I will get healthier," but "I AM getting healthier!" Pep talk is in the FIRST person: "I" not "You." Repeat the pep talk ten times. At the end, look at yourself, and say, "I'm pumped for the day. Hey life, BRING IT ON!"

2 minutes—Journal.

6 minutes—Watch TV for a few minutes and relax before my workout.

Analysis: I'm still focused on waking up without a hangover, and that's been my biggest challenge and success in the morning. I feel so much better and can now work out in the morning and feel more energized throughout the day. I figured learning to work out and be healthier was a great start for finding myself. What I didn't realize was this healthy living thing would become a burning passion inside of me that I'd never want to let go of. All we have in life is our health, and if we aren't healthy, we can't enjoy anything as much.

Also, adding a pep talk to my morning routine has been a game changer. Pumping myself up each morning for a minute or two helps me control my self-talk a lot more and keep myself focused on the positives I have to offer. It also helps destroy self-doubt! That is a huge reason I will continue giving myself pep talks each and every morning after I wake up.

I still have a lot of room for improvement, though, because I just kill time for 5-7 minutes in the morning aimlessly watching TV when I could be doing more productive things.

Chapter 5 – Goal Setting

"If you want to be happy, set a goal that commands your thoughts, liberates your energy and inspires your hopes."

~ Andrew Carnegie

As the first few weeks turned into the first few months of sobriety, I continuously saw changes in my lifestyle, my support system, and my body. Little did I know that in a few short months, my lifestyle changes would lead me to standing on a massive stage without my shirt on in front of hundreds of strangers competing for the right to be called "Mr. Pittsburgh."

My mornings still were my favorite part of my day and I continued to add other aspects to my morning routine. Thanks to my ability to attack my morning with purpose, energy, and a high-intensity workout, my body began to change. From the beginning of November 2011 till Christmas time, I dropped from 215 pounds to 197 pounds. A lot of the credit does go to my desire to work out in the morning, but I wouldn't have made as much progress if I hadn't quit drinking, started my First 15 minutes routine, and embraced eating much better.

The old saying goes, "You can't outwork a poor diet." It is absolutely true. For 10 years I tried to outwork a bad diet, and it got me nowhere. You'll see different experts say different percentages, but I think at least 80% of weight loss and getting healthier is diet and nutrition, and only 20% can be attributed to working out. No, that doesn't mean you don't have to work out! I'm not letting you off the hook that easily. But if the majority of your focus is on what is going down your throat, you will see a huge change in your energy and definitely in your waistband.

Again I give the credit to my good friend Chris Johnson at On Target Living for helping me create a nutrition plan that worked for me. I was so ready for a change in my life that I was able to quickly incorporate healthier options while deleting unhealthy foods and beverages from my diet. Most of the changes to my weight, energy, and overall outlook on healthy living came from my diet. Since the morning that I poured out all of those beers, I had only allowed healthier food and drink options inside my house. In fact, the only drink option I had in my house was water now. If that was the best drink for me, I figured, why would I have anything else?

For the first time in my life that I can remember, I physically wrote down specific goals I wanted to achieve for healthy living. I had goals like, "Don't put unhealthy food in the fridge," and "Do 30 minutes of cardiovascular workouts 3-4 times a week," and "Come up with a healthy lifestyle/eating plan with Chris Johnson and maintain it . . . forever." "Forever" was a key word because this wasn't some "get thin quick" fad I wanted. This was a lifestyle change that would make me healthier FOREVER! I scanned my goals every day right after I woke up to keep them fresh in my mind all day. Goal-setting was officially becoming a part of my First 15.

Chris helped me focus on eating 5–7 smaller meals per day, which helped my metabolism and also helped me to never feel stuffed with food or like I was starving. It was the perfect happy medium that my body and mind took to very well. My day from a nutrition standpoint now looked something like this:

5:30 am—Drink 8 oz. of water and eat a banana during my First 15

7:15 am—Post workout – plain Greek yogurt with berries, oats, and a little protein powder

10:30 am—Organic black beans with brown rice and broccoli

1:00 pm—Handful of almonds and raisins

3:30 pm—Grilled fish with olive oil and veggies

6:30 pm—three whole eggs and two egg whites with mushrooms and spinach plus whole wheat bread

8:30 pm—apple with organic peanut butter

*A lot of these foods can negatively affect someone with food allergies. Please consult a professional regarding a meal plan that may work best for your situation.

This is only an example of what I ate that worked well for me at this particular time in my life. I am not suggesting this same exact diet for everyone. Everyone's body is completely different, and age and genetics have a lot to do with your diet, so please make sure you know what you are doing, or consult someone in the medical field before changing a lot about your diet.

Around Christmas, I hadn't seen any of my four closest buddies in two months, and they stopped talking to me altogether because they knew I wasn't going back to that lifestyle. While losing friends isn't something I hoped would happen, it was an empowering feeling seeing that I left them in my rearview mirror to begin this better life for myself.

I remember the first time I went out to see my old friends after months of being away from them. I only decided to show up because one of my friends was celebrating a 30th birthday.

I walked into the bar pretty early into the party just so I could say my "hellos," wish him a happy birthday, and head out. Then, the questions started. "C'mon Scoletti, you aren't going to have ONE drink? It's a celebration!" This is the moment you have to remain strong if you want to have lasting change in your own life.

I thought about when I took that selfie and looked at myself in the mirror the day after Halloween and knew I couldn't go back to that space. I thought about what would happen if I had one drink, but I knew that I would have at least two, or three, or four more if I had that one. So I looked at my buddy, laughed, and said, "What are you talking about man? I'm going to drink a ton tonight! I already have my first water on the way! I'm driving, so I have to go easy." I like to use humor sometimes to combat peer pressure. And it worked. It got some laughs, and the conversation moved on to another topic.

But something else hit me that night about to my decision to leave this group of friends. Are my friends really that close to me if I have to keep defending changes I'm making in my life? No. I didn't think so. However, I was wondering if this was the good Lord giving me a little of what I had dished out years before. Remember, I had been an enabler, and I'm sure I offended some people who didn't want to spend the night slamming shot after shot as I egged them on to do another one. Now, it didn't feel great to get it in return. Please note, though, that I was not angry with my friends for pushing me to drink.

I was lucky that I found an amazing alternative to partying. Now, I spent many Friday and Saturday nights at 8 or 9 pm in my basement shadow boxing, doing pushups, and hitting my heavy bag. It was the perfect way to let out my frustrations about my old self or just have some fun getting a good sweat going. It was pure joy also because of the steps I had made to become healthier. I also liked that my workouts lasted much longer than the 15 minutes I lasted during my first attempt to work out in my basement.

As I blasted music on Friday and Saturday nights hitting the punching bag and shadow boxing, I kept envisioning the "old me" fading away with each swing of my fist. As he slowly faded, the "new me" started to emerge as this powerful, strong, and sober individual who was gaining more confidence by the day. Just writing this line gives me goosebumps because I go back to being in that basement and feeling the changes that were happening to my mind and body, and I loved every single moment of that.

I realized that getting rid of one habit was much easier if I substituted a new habit in its place. For example, I replaced nights of heavy partying with staying in and working out in my basement. I also replaced waking up with a hangover and stressed out many mornings with getting plenty of sleep and being productive first thing in the morning. I looked at it as taking out the garbage. I had a lot of garbage in my life, and every week or month I had to think of something else that was holding me back, and get rid of it.

Do you have any garbage in your life? I'm sure you have some trash that needs taken out and replaced. We all do! I challenge you to find a habit that is holding you back and replace it with a habit that will move you toward your goals and dreams! Take 5 minutes right now to write down a few habits that aren't productive, and then come up with new habits you can begin to form that will help you be your best. Go ahead and try it; I'll be here when you are finished.

Another thing I started to notice was that I started talking to and meeting many people who were into healthier living. How? Because you attract people who are like you. For example, I used to attract people who liked heavy drinking and late night partying, because that's what I did. Most of my friends were from meet ups at bars in my area. Now that I was waking up early, working out more, and getting involved in the fitness community, I started attracting healthier friends. I started meeting people at fitness events, in the gym, and on running trails. These friends enjoyed good clean foods, waking up early, crushing a morning workout, and making the most of each day.

I didn't know this was going to happen, nor did I predict it. This was a huge positive impact on my healthy living journey. If you decide to make a healthy shift in your life, and you lose your old friends like I did, I beg you to join groups on social media; meet people in the gym during a spin class, in adult sports leagues, obstacle course racing, yoga class, or many other places; and start to make connections with others who are getting healthier or are already healthy. That way, you'll not only build a great new group of friends, but you'll have people around you who live the lifestyle that you are attempting to live so they will automatically lift you up to be more like them.

If you are trying to make positive changes and don't have the support, please feel free to use me as a resource! Reach out to me at www.MattScoletti.com, and I'd love to help be a part of your progress to a healthier you! Almost everyone who is now healthy struggled for a period of time and can probably relate to you and help you along your journey. Build a support team that'll help bring you up in times when society is trying to beat you down.

In the beginning of my change, I had this "me against the world" mentality because I didn't know anyone else who was really healthy. I felt as if I had to constantly "defend" my healthy lifestyle. But it was more of an "old me vs. new me" power struggle that was going on for a while. All of this change clearly had me excited but also wondering how life would turn out for me now. That is why meeting new people and having an awesome healthy support system was awesome!

My buddy Marc became an accountability partner in the gym. We always saw each other there, and he would push me through tough workouts. He was also a personal trainer, so he knew a thing or two about working out. Marc was completely different from the friends I used to have. He encouraged me to keep eating the foods that would transform my body. He pushed me to stick with my values, knowing that my energy would keep increasing with each workout, good night's rest, and healthy meal.

As my body changed and my workouts got more intense, one day Marc said to the other trainers, "Try to train Scoletti. I dare you! His workout is so intense you can't come close to wearing him down."

I laughed. "I'm having the time of my life in the gym, what can I say? I'm learning how to make my body perform at its max capacity!"

Then Marc added, "I've never seen anyone enjoy an intense workout like you, my friend. Your work ethic is going to take you places for sure."

I appreciated all the encouragement Marc gave me, especially in front of the other trainers. I thought about his comment about my work ethic taking me far. I wasn't sure exactly how far it could take me, but I was excited to find out what was out there.

By March 2012, I looked completely different than I did on Halloween 2011. I was down to 175 pounds, having lost almost 40 pounds in 5 months. I still believe most of that weight was lost because I stopped binge drinking and eating garbage. My body was thanking me in the form of losing weight, and because I had been working out so much, I had added on a bunch of muscle. Or maybe I had the muscle the entire time, but now it showed because of my weight loss. Either way, I felt amazing!

For the first time in a decade, when I stepped out of the shower, I loved what I saw! I used to immediately put my shirt on after getting out of the shower to avoid having to look at my beer gut. Now, I actually took my time putting my shirt on and sometimes that was the very last thing I did in the morning because I couldn't believe what I was seeing. I had abs! Wow! I didn't quite have a 6-pack, but I had a nice little 4-pack going, and I felt amazing about the changes I saw. Plus, my energy had never been higher than it was now, and that got me just as excited as the physical changes.

After my alarm would go off in the morning, I would bounce out of bed because I knew that meant I got a chance to live, go after my healthy goals, do my current First 15, and lift weights in the gym. When you start to see the results like I did and feel the energy I had that early in the morning, it becomes an addiction that is stronger than alcohol or any drug that is out there! And I was so happy about it.

I also continued to learn different types of workouts while I was at the gym. I used to try to throw around as much weight as possible in the gym. Not anymore. I left that old me behind as well. That only increased my chance for injury, and I much preferred my new, high-intensity workouts that consisted of a ton of body weight exercises and relatively low weight for all of my lifting routines.

I refer to this style of lifting as cardio-weight training because it mixes the aerobic, heart pounding style of cardiovascular workouts with the strength training and muscle-building workouts. I'd also like to add (knock on wood), that this style of working out has never led me to get injured. Not once.

Another bonus: I met a few women while I was working out, partially from becoming somewhat more desirable because of my new physique, I guess. I'll take it! I wasn't ready for a girlfriend, but it was flattering to have some attention from the opposite sex. It never hurts to have that added motivation to change.

What was even more exciting about talking to the ladies in the gym was that I actually had the *confidence* to talk to them. Without even realizing it, I was becoming a more outgoing person while in the gym, and that was spilling out into the real world. I talked with a bunch of the trainers in the gym, took some spin and yoga classes where I met a lot of people, and was talking to a lot of gym regulars. My sobriety was starting to pay off, and my gym and First 15 routine were slowly turning me back into that outgoing person I was senior year of high school.

As I continued meeting people within the fitness community, I started going out on dates again. And even more exciting was that I was sober during these dates. Years before, I would drink 2–3 shots before meeting up with a girl for a date because of my nerves and lack of confidence. That was all changing as I kept pushing toward my healthy living goals. I didn't want to settle down yet, but I did enjoy getting back into the dating scene and also becoming more social with my new fitness friends.

Dating was one aspect of the social change, but I also started reconnecting with friends from years past who were in the process of getting healthier. These old friends coupled with some new people I had met in the fitness community became my new go-to social group.

While I was in these social settings, people rarely consumed any alcohol, and that was fine by me. That didn't stop our energy or silliness. It was wonderful! These were the type of people I wanted to continue to associate myself with.

Another part of my social change happened when I got the confidence to start a young adult volleyball league at our local church. I spoke to hundreds of people at the end of five church services and ended up attracting over 30 people to sign up. I never would have had the guts to attempt something like this just a couple years ago. The combination of my morning routine, goal setting, and healthy living helped me gain the confidence to make it happen! My sober social skills were back!

During my morning routines, I added in being thankful for the body that I now have and the new friends I was making. I finally found out that my body wasn't some old 27-year-old body and realized I have a lot of life left in me! It was a mentality that I never had in the past. Due to my positive, high energy morning routine, I felt as if I could conquer any workout or, really, anything! As you already know, it began to affect my social life as well as feeling more confident at work and doing presentations for different organizations I was associated with.

I mention this because it wasn't just my body getting healthier; my mind had seen the most improvement over these 5 months. Years prior, I couldn't even utter the word "cafeteria" to a stranger. But now I had filled my life with purpose and meaning, and as a result, my confidence began to increase quickly. I smiled constantly and started to feel more like the person that I was born to be.

I was still changing up my routine in the morning to better fit my style and help me feel my best before walking to the gym. Getting mentally prepared for my day in the morning is the most underrated concept I ever discovered. My workouts were so focused because I visualized myself being focused and had a game plan before walking through the doors of the gym. I knew what I wanted to accomplish during my 60-minute workout, and then once I got there, I executed my plan.

My job opening the gym in the morning ended after only 4 months because the owner retired and closed the gym. I found a new gym in the Pittsburgh-area though, and I didn't let the change throw off my newfound love for healthy living.

After a month at the new gym, I added a member to my new group of friends, and his name was Ali. He was a personal trainer at the gym I belonged to, and he had been following my progress in the gym. One day Ali walked up to me while I was working out and said, "I think you need to start competing with how great you look." I looked at him funny. "Competing? What does that mean?" Ali introduced me to bodybuilding, and more importantly, a new type of bodybuilding called "Physique."

I had to laugh. "I'm not about to go on stage in front of a bunch of people in a speedo, man, no way!"

So he cleared things up. He said Physique didn't mean I had to wear a speedo. "They wear regular swim trunks and look more like a beach guy with a good lean build. You'd be perfect for it, and I think we need to sign you up for the next show!" He had watched my body change over a short period of time and thought it would be a great way to keep me motivated and continue challenging myself.

I am so grateful that Ali came into my life at the right time. His Physique bodybuilding idea sounded like something totally out of my comfort zone, so I had to try it! I was so excited, and I relied on Ali to coach me through the process because he had competed on a big stage before.

I learned even more about the value of goal setting at this point of my life. I loved the idea of competing on the stage and set a goal to compete in my first show that May. My goal wasn't to *win* Mr. Pittsburgh because I know how subjective bodybuilding is, and it's possible to be the best one on stage and still not win. I didn't want to set a goal based on something I had no control over.

Instead, I set a goal to feel my best on stage! That was it. "Feeling my best" had many components, though. Many people who compete in these shows are completely miserable throughout the process because they restrict calories, eat zero carbs, and work out so much they have no time to enjoy anything. I didn't want to do any of that. My goal was to enjoy this process while also pushing myself to reach the healthiest point in my life both physically and mentally. That was the real goal. I wanted to see how fit I could get with my newfound passion for healthy living, and I wanted to be in better shape in my late 20s than I was when I was 17 years old!

As I trained, my amazing mornings continued! I was getting 8 hours of sleep each night, waking up, doing my current version of my

First 15, and then heading off to do a quick cardiovascular workout. After work, around 5:30 pm, I went to see Ali and crush a high-intensity, low-weight weightlifting session and discuss how to tweak my diet to get ready for my first Physique competition.

I was full of nervous excitement because, just 6 months before this, I was 30–40 pounds overweight and looked closer to a sumo wrestler than a Physique competitor! But just having the shot to be on stage with the best bodies and athletes in the entire East Coast of the United States was quite an accomplishment.

I signed up for the Mr. Pittsburgh Physique competition the following week. No backing out now! It was time for the final push with workouts, eating healthy, and making sure I felt my best coming into this huge show. I wasn't aware of this coming into the event, but 1,000 people would be there watching us, and I would be on stage with over 40 other competitors! This was insane! I couldn't believe I was doing this, but it was a monumental event in my life.

I don't think my parents quite knew what I was doing either. It's always interesting to start a conversation with your parents with, "Hey Mom and Dad, I'm going to take my shirt off for a bunch of strangers who paid money to come watch me." Ok, I didn't say it exactly like that, but I'm sure that's exactly what it sounded like to my parents. Their response was, "Wow that sounds interesting! Can we watch, too?"

My parents responded much better than I thought they would and were actually excited to watch me compete. Having my mom and dad support my desire to compete in this event meant so much. My brother supported me, too, but couldn't make it to this particular event because he was out of town. I think they all had noticed how my body and energy had changed over the last few months and wanted to be there for me.

I love my mom more than anything, and I idolize my dad and have always wanted to follow in his footsteps because he's that incredible of a human being. My dad has been an extremely successful businessman, while also giving a ton of time and money to many amazing charitable causes. He coached me in baseball and basketball growing up. He taught me about hard work, teamwork, dedication, and persistence. I thought if I did things similar to the way he did, I could be as happy and successful as he is. I definitely have his sense of humor, which is something I cherish because laughing together over silly things are some of my best memories with my Dad!

My mom has donated so much time to local charities and our church, so I was so blessed to have incredible role models in my own house growing up. I know I got the strength to change my entire lifestyle from my mom. She is tough as nails. And I know that because my brother and I still joke that she was the strictest mother in the whole world. But guess what . . . it worked! My mom instilled in me the power to stand up for myself even if others wouldn't, and I used this to help create massive change in my life. My mom never hesitates to speak up for what she feels is right and stick up for herself, and I used that gift from her to stick with my new values.

As you can imagine, when they wanted to support me in this fitness endeavor, I was so happy. I was grateful to have parents who wanted to cheer for me no matter what, especially if it was something they knew nothing about like this Mr. Pittsburgh event.

*****

May 4, 2012. The morning of the Mr. Pittsburgh show. The show that I had been working on my weight lifting, my diet, and my posing (yes, you have to pose like a beach boy with your hand on your hip while keeping your abs tight) for half a year. I tried to focus on my morning routine, while not letting the idea of being shirtless in front of 1,000 people keep creeping into my mind.

What I learned about competing was that I couldn't just throw on a pair of board shorts and walk on stage. Oh no! Many other things had to happen first. I had to get a spray tan and was forced to shave off the majority of my body hair, which wasn't something I was looking forward to. But, I had already signed up for the contest, so I shaved my legs, chest, arms, back, and anywhere else that you might see if I'm wearing a pair of shorts. I did learn something important about myself, though: I had hair in areas that I never thought was possible!

Then, I was off to get a spray tan, and I couldn't believe how dark this made me look. The spray tan lady told me that the lights on stage would make me look "normal." That's how "not normal" I looked at that point. Speaking of "not normal," my bedsheets looked like the mob scene from *The Godfather* when I woke up the day after the event because the spray tan bled all over them. I expected to see a horse's head at the foot of my bed. Make sure to shower more thoroughly than I did if you ever get a spray tan.

As I continued to feel more and more nervous on competition day, I tried to take a step back and smile at the progress I had made. For 10 years, I hadn't done anything that required the motivation and self-discipline that this did. What an accomplishment, and I hadn't even stepped on stage yet.

I had my spray tan rocking, I had my board shorts on for the show, and it was close to time to hit the stage. That meant I had to go to the "pump up room." This was the point in the day where I had to make it look like I knew what I was doing, even though I felt completely out of place since this was my first attempt at something like this.

When I walked in, I saw at least 200 male and female athletes who were spray tanned, had 0.1% body fat on them, and smelled awful because everyone was doing pushups, using resistance bands, and trying other techniques to make their muscles "pop," or stick out more. I laughed and made a "wow this smells so bad" face. Everyone knew how bad it smelled, but I had some fun being vocal about the rancid stench. This helped me loosen up before it came time to line up and get ready to step on stage.

I will never forget being number "33" that day. Over 500 athletes took the stage that evening at Soldiers and Sailors Hall in Pittsburgh, PA, with over 40 competitors in the Physique Division. I just hoped I would place in the top half of the competitors. Actually, I didn't even care about that because of the progress I'd made in my life. I just couldn't wait to get on stage, feel that rush of energy, and see how I felt being shirtless and judged in front of 1,000 people.

It was exciting that no matter what position I finished in, I was officially in the best physical and mental shape of my life at 29 years old! What a victory before even going on stage and being judged!

As I stood behind the curtain, waiting for the announcer to call my name, I enjoyed the rush of energy I felt. The announcer said "Number 33, from the Southside of Pittsburgh...Matt...Scoletti." I don't remember the next 60 seconds of my life, but apparently, I was hamming it up with the audience, smiling, and giving some nice poses out in the middle of the stage. I was nervous and energized, but I appeared calm.

After all the Physique competitors were on stage, the judges analyzed each of us and announced their top five selections in random order. I heard, "Number 193 to the front." I wasn't really paying attention because I figured I had a 0% chance of being called. "Number 408." "Number 118." "Number 334 to the front." I knew it. Good for these 4 guys because they look great, and that's probably who I would have selected. "And finally, number 33." WHAATTT? ME? Number 33? I must have looked down at my number 4 or 5 times to make sure it actually read "33" on it. It did! It did say 33! I couldn't believe it.

There I stood, in the center of a huge auditorium in the biggest Physique show in the entire Northeast, and I was in the top five overall! And this was my FIRST SHOW EVER! Six months ago I was waking up on my living room floor, spending the first 15 minutes of my morning trying to figure out if I should throw up in the kitchen sink, or if I could make it up to the bathroom. And now? Wow! I couldn't wrap my head around my progress yet! It was overwhelming.

Three minutes later, I found out that I won 2nd place overall in the Mr. Pittsburgh competition! I held that massive trophy and smiled out at the audience. I smiled, and I also become slightly emotional because of my story. The last 10 years flashed in front of my eyes in 5 seconds. I thought about my out-of-control drinking, friends I had gained and lost, relationships I had, and my support system of more and more healthy people. My life felt right. Things were going in the right direction for the first time in a decade. I wanted this. And I didn't want to stop being healthy. That is the one thing I knew for sure.

After I got my trophy, I went up to see my parents in their seats. They were overjoyed! My dad, being the strong supporter that he was, and slightly biased, said "I think you should have had him son. The guy who won looked good, but clearly, you should be holding that first place trophy." If you couldn't tell, my Dad is competitive. I guess that's where I get it from. I could have been standing next to Arnold Schwarzenegger in his prime, and he would say, "He looked halfway decent, but you looked 100 times better!"

I saw Ali on the way downstairs, and he gave me a huge hug! "You looked unbelievable out there!" he said. "I'm so happy you listened to your wise friend who said you should compete on stage. Wow, that was a smart guy for suggesting that to you." We both laughed, and I said, "Yes, but didn't my wise friend say I was going to win?" He laughed even harder and assured me that this was only the beginning of my Physique competition success.

Following the 2nd place award (which was a trophy that was almost as tall as I was) at Mr. Pittsburgh in 2012, I couldn't believe my momentum. I loved the feeling of getting into the best shape of my life and then presenting myself on stage to large group of people. I was addicted to this new lifestyle, and I wanted more and more and more.

I ended up competing in four different shows in 2012 and taking two second place trophies and two first place trophies! I won my first show in the middle of 2012, and it was an incredible feeling. I ended up coming back and winning Mr. Pittsburgh in the spring of 2013, which was an incredible experience!

I feel obligated to tell you something else. My body was (and IS) 100% natural during all my competitions. I have never taken a steroid to enhance my performance in my life, and I would never put anything like that in my body. The only supplement I take besides a multivitamin is protein powder, and that is only on occasion as I get most of my nutrition from natural foods.

My goals also changed during this string of Physique shows I competed in. First, I just wanted to get into good enough shape to get on stage for the Mr. Pittsburgh show. After that, I had a goal of becoming the healthiest male in Pittsburgh. That was a vague goal, but it helped keep me motivated, so I figured it was working. I wanted to prove that a natural athlete can be on the same stage as someone who was taking steroids by making sure I was getting a good amount of exercise mixed with amazing nutrition and a ton of rest.

After doing so well in those four shows around Pittsburgh in 2012, I was awarded the Physique Athlete of the Year! I was the best Physique athlete in the entire Northeast that year according to the National Physique Committee. I couldn't believe it when I got the phone call to accept the award. As I listened to the man tell me about this award and congratulate me on this miraculous run of Physique events in 2012, I couldn't believe all that had happened. I also couldn't believe that I set out to be the healthiest man in all of Pittsburgh, and now this man was telling me that I was the most fit man in the entire Northeast of the country! I felt like the most blessed man in the entire world and that was a feeling that I didn't want to go away. It all happened because I began to conquer the first 15 minutes of my day!

One of the most interesting parts of this journey was the transformation in how people were treating me. The friends who once laughed at my healthy food choices and scoffed at my early nights and even earlier mornings were now asking me how I got myself into great shape so they too could get healthier. But I wasn't upset with them. I smiled and was honored that they came around and understood exactly why I changed my lifestyle.

Life had certainly changed for me. Learning about goal setting throughout this Mr. Pittsburgh process had a profound effect on me. Everyone has heard about setting goals, but until I actually did it, I didn't believe it. The other thing that was weird was that all the goals I set for myself actually became reality. Seeing my goals written out was a huge motivator because they became much more real to me. Without goals, my life was just like a rudderless ship: I had no direction. But by setting goals and reviewing them every morning, I could focus my energy on exactly what I wanted, and then go out there and attack it. It works!

After having such success in the Physique competitions and in the goal-setting process, I figured reviewing my goals would be paramount during the First 15 morning routine. I wanted to make sure this goal-setting practice was ongoing and something I continued to review and update far after my competitions in Physique.

*****

Current First 15:

5 minutes—WAKE UP! "Yes, I get to play again!" Stretch, water, water, snack.

2 minutes—Goals. Review/update goals! This helps keep them fresh in your mind and keeps you motivated! Having goals, and writing down exactly when and how I wanted to become Mr. Pittsburgh made it feel attainable and real! Goals are dreams with deadlines, and they work! Looking at them every day is an extremely powerful way to start your day.

How to do it: Use a goals sheet that has categories on it like "financial," "spiritual," "health," and "community" (more on this in section 2). Take a few minutes to figure out what goals you want to accomplish in what about of time, and make sure they are specific. Then, each morning for a minute or so, take a look at your goals sheet so they stay fresh in your head. That way, you'll know where you are headed and how to get yourself to reach those goals. This process will help you lead a more fulfilled and ambitious life!

2 minutes—Journal a little

4 minutes—Check social media, read texts from previous night, watch some TV

1 minute—Pep Talk!

The First 15

1 minute—Play upbeat music to get me excited about the workout

Analysis: The First 15 Routine continues to improve, but I'm still not being productive during part of it. It's so exciting that I'm still journaling and learning about myself through that technique. I also made a huge improvement by reviewing my goals and possibly adding more goals to my list. It's amazing what looking at my goals for 1–2 minutes each morning can do to keep me motivated, inspired, and ready to conquer the day! It's also exciting because I know there is a lot of room for improvement on my First 15.

Chapter 6 – Laughter is Essential to Your Health

"What soap is to the body, laughter is to the soul."

~ Yiddish Proverb

As 2012 continued to roll right along for me, I loved my morning workouts, jumping out of bed, and being thankful that I got to play in the world again! My current First 15 helped me get that whoosh in the morning that got me even more excited to hit the gym. What an incredible feeling and such a change from the prior year . . . and prior 10 years!

The more I stepped on stage, and the more people found out that I was becoming successful in the Physique world, the more people followed me on my social media pages. As a result, I wanted to give more and more material for people to follow along on my journey. I wanted to show my followers exactly what I was going through as I trained and prepared to keep my body in tip-top shape, and I felt important because some people were in awe of my workouts and their intensity.

I didn't have a plan when I started posting pictures and videos of my workouts and my progress, but I decided to start doing it anyway. My videos were just supposed to be something easy to follow to help people get different workout ideas, but I admit, it was also to keep myself motivated and excited about the progress I had made in life.

I showed a couple of the videos to my mom, but she wasn't impressed. She said I wasn't being myself, and I needed to show some enthusiasm. She was right. Looking back on those videos now, I looked about as excited as someone listening to a sales pitch for aluminum siding. I could have looked up "funeral ceremony video" and seen more excitement than my videos showed.

It killed me to hear my mom make those comments because I'm one of the most enthusiastic individuals that I know! But when the camera was on, for some reason, I changed. So I practiced more and tried to get myself to show my true colors. Eventually, it worked because friends and followers actually started watching the videos.

I enjoyed the challenge of being myself on camera. Doesn't that sound funny just reading it? It was a "challenge" to "be myself." So weird, but it was so true. Ralph Waldo Emerson once said, "To be yourself in a world that is constantly trying to make you something else is the greatest accomplishment." I held onto this quote and continued to not only find my true self, but also *be* my true self in real life and on camera.

Then, one video changed the way I thought of myself. It truly changed my life.

One afternoon, I had planned to do a video to show my viewers the correct way to use a resistance band while doing bicep curls. I stood on the resistance band with my arms hanging down to my sides, and while holding one side of the resistance band in each hand, I began to move my right hand toward my shoulder in a bicep curl. The camera was rolling, and I started to say, "You can even do bicep curls—" when SNAP! My foot slipped off the bottom of the resistance band, and the band went flying toward my head and cracked my cheek hard.

I yelled, "Oh my God, oh my God, aahhhhhh!" My cheek felt like it was on fire. I held the side of my face and just felt lucky that it didn't hit me in the eye. I took the camera off of the stack of boxes and watched the video to make sure I deleted the right one and destroyed the evidence.

But as the video ran, I couldn't help but laugh at the precision of that band seeking out the perfect place to strike. BAM! Just before I pressed delete, though, I thought, "I need to replay that. This is too funny!" As I watched over and over again, I wondered if I should post it on my website and social media.

I wasn't sure if I should because it was embarrassing, but it was so funny.

Side note: I couldn't film any more videos that day because the whole side of my face turned bright red. I wouldn't have needed a mask to dress up as the Batman villain Two-Face that day.

I decided to post the video. I had two other funny outtakes that I posted along with the resistance band to the face video clip to make a mini outtakes video of about 30 seconds. The video exploded on social media. I got the most joy out of making other people smile, and if it had to come at my own expense, then so be it. This part of my life helped me realize that laughing had to be a daily activity. And I'm not talking about a giggle. I needed an all-out belly laugh at least once a day for me to be happy. This video and social media response helped me belly laugh constantly for weeks!

Almost immediately after I posted the video, people were commenting and loving the montage of my screw ups. One guy commented, "LOL. You better send that in to *America's Funniest Home Videos*! Classic!"

I sat at my computer laughing and began to think he was right. Maybe I *should* send it in. I also laughed because apparently a lot of people enjoy watching me take painful slaps to my face courtesy of resistance bands.

I quickly went to *America's Funniest Home Videos'* website. I uploaded the montage and laughed as it showed up for me to preview. "Click." And just like that, it was sent to the show.

A few weeks after posting my funny video to *America's Funniest Home Videos'* website, I got a call from a California number as I was driving across a bridge on my way home from work. "Hello, this is Katie from *America's Funniest Home Videos*, how are you this afternoon?"

I almost dropped the phone. "Hi Katie, how are you today?"

"I'm doing great. I just wanted to give you a call to congratulate you on being picked to have your video on our show!"

"What? Really? Katie, don't joke around with me now. I'm on a bridge, and I don't want to hurt myself here!"

She laughed and said "No, I mean it. We all loved your video and want to have it on our show!"

I did need to pull over after I got off the bridge because I was starting to breath heavy. "Katie, are you sure you are looking for me: Neil Tomlinson?"

She sounded confused when she said, "Oh wait. Is this Matt? I'm so sorry."

I laughed. "Yes, this is Matt. I got you though, didn't I?" I had to hold the phone away from my ear because she was laughing so hard.

"With jokes like that, you'd make a perfect addition to our show, Matt. We would like you to be here to watch your clip air on TV!" I wasn't sure I understood and asked what she meant. "Your video was selected as a Top 3 candidate, and we are inviting you and a guest to fly out to Los Angeles for three nights, come to the taping of the show, and sightsee around LA after the taping. All expenses paid of course. How does that sound?"

"This...is...awesome! My stupidity is finally paying off!" She laughed again and commented that it might *really* pay off because the 1st place video gets $5,000, 2nd place gets $3,000, and 3rd place gets $2,000. She again asked what I thought. "Katie, you had me at 'free trip to Los Angeles'! I can't believe there is prize money involved too! I'm in! I can't wait!"

I hung up and drove back to my house. Then I sat on a swinging chair in my backyard and cried happy tears. I didn't cry because I was finally getting paid for being an idiot. I cried because, for the first time since high school, I decided to put myself out there and take some risks. I decided to get out of my comfort zone and film fitness videos that anyone could see.

I cried because of all of the changes I made to my lifestyle over the last year—my one-year sober anniversary was the next month. I thought about waking up hungover so many times on my living room floor, and then I cried because I knew those days were over. I was on a better path now, one I would stick with. *This* was the life I wanted.

I also cried because I finally had some values. For the first time in in my life, I stood up for something. I took a stand in my life and fought my alcoholism. I completely reinvented who I was and changed how I felt about myself. I took a stand in my life to change the first 15 minutes of my morning, which snowballed through the rest of my day, the rest of my year, and the rest of my life.

If I slacked a little in that First 15, I wasn't as productive that day and felt like I missed out on growing as a person. Even if I didn't have a full 15 minutes, I always made sure to do something in the morning to jumpstart my day, even for only 2–5 minutes.

Receiving that call from *America's Funniest Home Videos* was a powerful moment. After that, I was on a high like I can't even describe. It was like I had "made it" in life. And this moment was triggered because of a funny, slightly pathetic video that would now be seen by millions of people across the United States. Funny how life works, right? I had to laugh that night because I knew this was who I was put on this planet to be. I was a funny, slapstick-loving, high-energy, emotional, crazy healthy living guy who loved to constantly laugh and poke fun at myself. To most people, this video just looked like a silly 10-second clip. But for me, it encapsulated my love for laughter, positivity, workouts, energy, and/or life all in one ridiculous outtake.

A few weeks later, my brother and I were on a flight to Los Angeles to spend three glorious nights sightseeing and enjoying the 2–3 hour taping of *America's Funniest Home Videos*. It was just a three-night trip, and it was because of a screw up video that some people from *AFV* enjoyed, right? That's all it would be to many people. But to me, it was one million times more important! It was a celebration of my healthy living stance, and I was so proud of the improvement I had made in my life over the last 18 months. That's what this trip meant to me.

The First 15

The morning of the taping of the show, my brother and I got to the studio about an hour before the audience could go in. The other two contestants seemed nervous. They didn't talk much before the taping began. But my brother and I were loose and excited, laughing with the staff and other contestants because it didn't matter to me who won: I felt I already had. Fine, I kind of take that back. Of course I wanted to win! But I was still relaxed and enjoying the moment!

It turns out that my video of getting hit in the face with the resistance band actually took second place, so I didn't win. It stunk to not take home the first prize, but my brother and I had a great time anyway because we got to explore Malibu, Hollywood, Venice Beach, and many other sights in Los Angeles, plus I was going home with $3,000. Not bad for a guy who just happened to send in a funny video a month prior!

The following weekend, I was sitting on my back porch again, thinking about how so much of my life had already changed in just over a year. To me, *America's Funniest Home Videos* became a validation that I was turning my life in the right direction. It was more than just a stupid video on TV. I got out of my comfort zone and began filming videos of myself to teach others about healthy living. That was something I had never done before.

I got *way* out of my comfort zone by actually sending the video to the show. Then, to be picked out of the hundreds or thousands of videos they receive just made everything so awesome. I sometimes debated whether I should go back to bar hopping and living the life I used to live with a ton of "friends" and not having a care in the world. But, with this experience and my new love for the first 15 minutes of my day and healthy living, I couldn't wait for what was in store next.

*****

Current First 15:

5 minutes—WAKE UP! "Yes, I get to play again!" Stretch, water, water, snack.

2 minutes—Goals. Review/update goals!

2 minutes—Journal a little. Sometimes write in my journal, sometimes not. I actually started writing in my journal more at night during this time and not as much in the morning. Before, I couldn't write in my journal at night because I was normally drunk. I now enjoy a peaceful 5 minutes of journaling before bed. I write in my journal about the day, the goals for the next day, and my feelings. This was about the time I officially took journaling out of my morning routine and added it to my nightly ritual.

1 minute—Laugh! If I learned anything from this experience, it is that we need to laugh every single day! A day without laughing is a wasted 24 hours. So I will make it a point to laugh at something (or myself) in the first 15 minutes of each day! Laughter is the best medicine right? So why not take the best medicine every morning within 15 minutes of waking up? You have to!

How to do it: Either make faces at yourself in the mirror until you laugh or just "fake laugh" until that turns into a real laugh. Trust me; it works! Give it a try! It's a great way to get out of your comfort zone early in the morning too! Another option is to recall something that makes you laugh every time it pops into your mind. Use whatever it takes to get you laughing each morning.

3 minutes—Check social media, read texts from previous night, watch some TV

1 minute—Pep Talk!

1 minute—Play upbeat music to get me excited about the workout

Analysis: I'm still learning what is the best way to start my day, but my mornings continue to be very productive. It's exciting to have a great routine starting to come together.

Journaling has become more of a night activity now, which is ok because I have to do whatever routine is the best for me. Laughing in the morning within a few minutes of waking up feels incredible. I want to continue doing that for the rest of my life! Laughing is always something I've cherished, so it's a solid part of my morning routine now. I'm still wasting a few minutes before my workout as I check social media or occasionally flip on the TV, so I'm working to stop that altogether in my morning routine. I want my full 15 minutes to be productive in the morning, and the social media/TV watching is just filler time, which wasn't productive or necessary.

Chapter 7 – Gratefulness and Visualization are so Powerful

"The best way to find yourself, is to lose yourself in the service of others."

~ Mahatma Gandhi

I had reached the top! Or so I thought. My mornings were amazing! I worked out every morning, I stayed sober, and I felt like I was on top of the world. I had won Mr. Pittsburgh and became the Physique Athlete of the Year. I had become a spokesman for a supplement company and a sponsored athlete with On Target Living, and I didn't think life could get much better. But something was still missing.

Turning my life completely around was one of the most rewarding experiences ever. I take that back. It was THE MOST rewarding experience of my life! Until that point. I remember the feeling of pure joy as I stood on the stage and won Mr. Pittsburgh, and I felt like I was breaking through and crushing my goals that I set for myself. The key word was "myself."

This lifestyle change was something that I absolutely did for myself. I needed to get myself in the right mindset and learn which values I wanted to live by. But I was missing something I had a passion for: helping other people. I had always enjoyed volunteering my time and doing my best to put a smile on others' faces. In this chapter, I talk about what led to the greatest weekend of my entire life!

I had been dating Steph (I refer to her as Chef Steph quite a bit because her cooking is so awesome and healthy!) for about 2 years, and clearly she was the one for me! It didn't take long into our dating for me to realize this was one special woman. She was a leukemia survivor who was diagnosed at 19 years old.

The one story that sums up Chef Steph to perfection comes from the doctor who had to give her the news of her cancer. He tells the story, "I remember seeing the diagnosis and having to tell this poor 19-year-old girl about it. When I told her, she didn't get mad or sad. She looked at me with this smile that could light up a whole country and said, 'What do we do now, Doctor?' And Stephanie smiled every single morning I went to see her. It was the most uplifting leukemia case I'd ever seen, and this girl was a true warrior throughout her battle." Steph has a smile that can make you forget about any problems you may have had that day. It's that radiant and powerful!

Steph used her battle with leukemia to take a heroic stance against cancer and support other young adults who are battling the disease. She started Young Adult Cancer Support (YACS), which gives other young adults a place to share their story and help one another during monthly support groups.

Steph also raises money for YACS to cover the cost of one social gathering a month so the survivors can do something that takes their minds off of their chemotherapy, treatment, or anything else relating to cancer. Plus, she gives grants to members who are struggling to pay for their cancer treatments and medical bills. Steph is a force for good in this world and an incredible leader! I knew that my passion for helping others needed to be fulfilled through her YACS group because they were all fighting a tough battle.

Because I was dating Steph, I attended many socials with the YACS group. Before the first social, I remember thinking, "I wonder if everyone will have no energy and look sick. They probably won't want to say much to me because I don't have cancer and don't understand." How ignorant and naive of me. I walked into the social and couldn't believe the energy! These young people, some of whom just had chemotherapy the day before, were full of energy, full of humor, and full of life! They refused to let a disease stop them from living their lives and fighting. What an inspiration! I know not everyone diagnosed with cancer has a positive outcome, but it was nice to see everyone supporting each other no matter the severity of their diagnosis.

In December of 2013, I told Steph that I wanted to raise money for YACS. I decided to enter the World's Toughest Mudder in November of 2014. This event is a 5-mile obstacle course in Las Vegas that competitors attempt to complete as many times as possible in a 24-hour period. But unlike the Mr. Pittsburgh competition, which I did solely for my own fulfillment, I raised the stakes to fulfill my love for fitness challenges and my love for helping others. There was no better group to help than Steph's YACS group.

This was my vision: In January of 2014, I would sign up for this insane fitness event, often called "the toughest event on the planet." I would train my rear end off all year and call, email, and connect with people I knew, asking them to donate a certain dollar amount PER MILE that I completed on the course. If people donated per mile completed, then my performance would directly correlate to the amount of money raised, which would give me more incentive to do well! My goal was to complete over 30 miles on the course and raise $10,000.

By April of 2014, my vision was becoming reality. I started telling people about what I was doing and—after telling me that I was completely insane for entering the event—most decided to help out. My heart and body were filled with warmth throughout this whole process. That summer I had people from close family members and friends to individuals I hadn't spoken to in years tell me they would donate to this amazing cause! I couldn't have been more excited to wake up each morning because attempting to raise over $10,000 and to push my body to the absolute max in the World's Toughest Mudder was truly fulfilling.

Something else happened while I was securing donors for YACS. I continued to gain confidence in myself, not only with my physical capabilities, but with my mental, social, and emotional strength, as well. I was holding meetings to pitch my idea to potential donors, and calling people out of the blue to ask for sponsorships for the event. I pushed myself so far out of my comfort zone that it helped me grow even more as a person.

I learned that staying in my comfort zone would never help me grow as an individual. I needed to keep challenging myself physically, mentally, and socially so I could become the person that I dreamed of being. This was a huge transformation from years prior when I would run away from a challenge. With my new confidence, I wanted to take on different challenges that were presented to me. I have a drinking cup with the quote "Life begins at the end of your comfort zone" on it, and I completely agree. If you never get out of your comfort zone, life will never change, and you'll never be able to experience what you are truly capable of.

As summer turned into fall, the donation pledges kept rolling in, my training was going extremely well, and my relationship with my girlfriend Steph couldn't have been better. It was so good that I told my parents that I planned to ask Steph to marry me in November 2014 . . . two days before the World's Toughest Mudder. They love Steph, so they were overjoyed and couldn't have been happier with my decision for who I wanted to spend the rest of my life with.

I'm the type of person that doesn't mind doing a bunch of rather important things in a short amount of time, such as proposing to my girlfriend on a Thursday night in Las Vegas, and then taking on the biggest fitness event of my life two days later. I couldn't help it: I was so excited and never had this much energy in my life! WHAT A WEEKEND THIS WAS GOING TO BE!

As my training continued into fall, I felt like my body was in the best shape it possibly could be in. My only concern was a minor knee injury during training in September, which caused me to miss a full marathon I had signed up for. I listened to my body, though, by resting in September and ramped it back up in early October, building my cardiovascular strength and refining my diet to make sure both were under control prior to the November 14th event.

I tallied up the donations a few days before leaving for Las Vegas and realized if I did over 25 miles, we would reach our goal of raising over $10,000 for YACS. That was a huge motivator for me, and I had all the survivors of YACS in my corner cheering me on from Pittsburgh! What a thrill it was to have these amazing people getting so excited about my challenge . . . not to mention on Thursday I would be asking my girlfriend to marry me.

On the morning of Thursday, November 12th, Steph and I stood in the airport waiting to board our plane. I met a man there, Rob, was also competing in the World's Toughest Mudder, so we discussed our strategies for attacking the course. When I got to my seat on the plane, I was surprised to see that Rob was right across the aisle. Steph sat in front of me because we couldn't get seats next to each other on the flight. I talked to Rob a lot during the flight and got a brilliant idea.

I wrote a quick note and passed it across the aisle so Steph wouldn't hear my plan. It said, "I know this sounds weird, but I'm proposing to my girlfriend in the baggage claim of the airport, do you think you could videotape it on your phone?" I'm sure others on the plane thought I was sending this man love letters or something, but I didn't care what they thought because this would be amazing if we pulled it off!

The plan was to get off the plane and meet up with a limo driver I had hired to pick us up at the airport. He would be holding a sign that said "Stephanie Samolovitch," and as we approached, he would flip over the sign, which said "Will you marry me?" on the back. By the time Steph looked back at me, I'd be on my knee. It sounded perfect, right? Well, curveballs always seem to happen during marriage proposals.

The plane landed, and Steph and I headed to baggage claim. As my heart raced, I kept saying, "I love you so much, Honey. I just love you so much." After the seventh or eighth time, she shot me the "what is wrong with you" look. By then, though, we were standing right in front of the limo driver.

Steph looked at the sign and said, "What is going on? That's me. I'm so confused. Who got this for us?" I nodded to the limo driver as if to say, "Turn the sign around," but he didn't budge. I kept faking like I was going to drop to my knee, but that didn't make him move either. If you watch the video, which can be viewed on YouTube if you search "WTM Airport Proposal," you'll see my "fake knee" about 3–4 times. He still didn't flip the sign. *WHAT IS GOING ON?* (Later, I found out I was supposed to give him a thumbs up when he needed to turn it. Clearly I messed that up).

After what felt an hour (in reality maybe 10 seconds), the limo driver finally turned the sign. Steph said, "OH MY GOD!" and gave me a huge hug! "Oh my God" doesn't qualify as a "yes," but don't worry, I confirmed her answer shortly after. What a start to the weekend!

We spent the rest of the night riding around in the limo (and calling our families!) to the famous Las Vegas sign and the Bellagio fountains, and finally, we had dinner atop the Eiffel Tower restaurant that overlooks the Las Vegas Strip. It was truly MAGICAL. We were engaged!

The following day (the day before the big event) Steph and I were still on Cloud 109, and she was still shocked from the proposal. But we were also busy running around Las Vegas getting food, clothes, and other items we would need to survive this race! While I was competing, Steph would remain in an area called "The Pit"—about 1,000 tents in the middle of the desert where competitors could fuel back up after each 5 miles completed. Athletes could also stretch out, nap, or do whatever was possible to keep their mind and body nourished and fresh for another 5-mile lap.

I'd like to say I got 2 hours of sleep the night before World's Toughest Mudder, but that might be an exaggeration. I never had so much nervous energy—part of it probably still from proposing to the woman of my dreams—in my life! I couldn't contain myself. In the morning, I ate a huge breakfast in the hotel, and then began to get dressed. I only needed shorts and a workout shirt to begin the event because it would be 55–60° F outside.

After I slid on my race bib, we wrote "YACS" across my chest so Steph and I would remember why I was doing this race. This event was for all those young adults back home battling cancer. I got emotional as I looked at myself with "YACS" across my chest. Then, I smiled at my fiancé and said, "I've been waiting years to do something like this. LET'S CRUSH IT!"

The scene at the event was incredible. Right in the middle of the rolling hills of the desert were these insane obstacles, thousands of people, and hundreds of tents. As we walked closer, carrying a ton of food, drinks, and clothes for when the weather would turn cold, I saw a massive 50-foot platform in the distance, which was an obstacle called "The Cliff." At over 4 stories high, towering over Lake Las Vegas, this obstacle tested your mental strength to just jump and go for it!

In "The Pit" area, excitement, nervousness, and pure insane energy oozed out of each athlete, and it was awesome to see! Everyone was talking about the course and what their strategy was on water, food, stretching, and doing their best to last for 24 hours, especially given the unpredictability of the desert weather.

We put our stuff down in our Pit area, and I chatted with my friend Giovanni, who I'd be attacking the course with. Giovanni was slightly taller than me with a lean build and was in great shape. We initially connected on social media. As that connection swelled into a friendship, we had agreed to stick together during the entire race, picking each other up when down and forcing ourselves to push our bodies to the limit. Remember when I mentioned surrounding yourself with people who will help lift you up? This is exactly what Giovanni did for me, and I could tell right away that we had formed a special bond that would last well beyond this race! His dad and good friend were there supporting him as his Pit Crew. Giovanni, his dad, his buddy, Steph, and myself were about to begin a 24-hour adventure like no other on the planet, and I couldn't wait!

The First 15

I looked around and saw nothing but tents all around me, hundreds of them, and then "The Cliff" off in the background and the mountains of the desert hovering over the Pit ominously. It was everything I imagined it would be for an event called "World's Toughest Mudder." I looked into the eyes of the other men and women who I'd be spending the next 24 hours with, and they showed excitement, determination, worry, and intensity. With 25 of the toughest obstacles on the planet coming up, I'm sure many of us would be bloody, have minor injuries, cramp up, and feel insane fatigue. I just hoped everyone would remain safe and all battle wounds would heal quickly after the race.

As Steph and I approached the starting line, I felt like a soldier going into battle. I knew for the next 24 hours, my mind and body would be pushed further than ever before. I was nervous, and my body was tight. But I knew that would soon go away, so I kept chugging water to stay hydrated longer. The hype guy for World's Toughest Mudder gave an amazing speech about never giving up and being your best. I had goosebumps the entire time. After his speech, as over 1,000 Mudders stood together, the American flag was raised, and the national anthem played.

That's when the reality of the magnitude of this event hit me. The flag flying high and our nation's anthem playing was always something I cherished. I usually tear up just hearing the national anthem and remembering all the soldiers who fought for the right to allow me to live in a free country. It blows my mind that individuals were willing to make those sacrifices for people they didn't even know. I felt that intense respect for our military and country like never before in this emotional moment of my life. As the cool breeze unfurled the flag perfectly, each note of the "Star Spangled Banner" thumped into my heart with unparalleled power.

I looked at my fiancé who was about 30 feet away outside of the competitor ropes, and we both had tears in our eyes. We also both had huge smiles on our faces. I was emotional for many reasons, including the battle I'd been through internally with alcohol and lack of confidence for years. I allowed myself to not be my best version of me, and I used to get in my own way constantly, which denied me a successful life. Not anymore!

Being able to support those young adults battling cancer by doing something I love made me shed tears of joy. I would give them my all for the next 24 hours. I loved each and every one of them and admired their attitudes in the face of cancer. That is being a true badass!

My tears were also for the love of my life who stood by me through everything. She supported my training for months, freezing her butt of on my multiple camping adventures that fall as I did training runs for this event. She supported me being crazy enough to want to run through the desert for 24 hours and enter one of the most dangerous events on the planet. She was my rock, my one true love, my fiancé, and in a little over a year...my wife! I couldn't wipe the smile off my face as she stood there looking so gorgeous in her workout pants, pit bib, and that smile, oh that smile that could light up an entire city! I gave her a wink and mouthed the words "I love you so much." She did the same back to me. What a moment between the two of us! It was beautiful, loving, and emotion-filled, and I'll never forget it.

Have you ever had a moment in your life that was so profound and perfect that you could put yourself right back into that situation if you just closed your eyes? I bet you have! If I'm ever having a tough day, I just think about this moment between me and my wife and feel it with all my heart. It instantly makes me feel better. Try this with your amazing moment also. Feel your heart warm up because of how another person or event made you feel. Use this if you are ever having a bad day and need a pick-me-up.

The gun went off at 10:00 am, starting 24 hours of fun and hell. I was shoulder to shoulder with some of the greatest athletes in the world who would push themselves to the limit. Being part of such an elite group of athletes was inspiring, especially because everyone wanted to do their best but also help others along the way.

If someone couldn't get over a wall, someone else would lend them a hand and help them over. If someone was getting down on themselves, someone else would give them a pep talk to lift their spirts. The Tough Mudder community is incredible, and anyone who has done a Tough Mudder knows what I mean. We respect and love our fellow competitors, and even though we all want to be the best, we also don't want to let anyone fail. Tough Mudders will sacrifice their time and energy to help someone over that wall or through the mud or to motivate them to jump off a 50-foot platform into water.

Giovanni and I soon found out that the 5-mile course was laced with obstacles like 20-foot walls to climb, modified monkey bars that were 10 times as difficult as normal monkey bars, and endless hills to mount.

The obstacle with the biggest crowd of onlookers was The Cliff. We had to jump off it into the water below, and the fans enjoyed watching people take the plunge. This was such a mental obstacle, and looking over the side of The Cliff was definitely terrifying, but like in life, you just have to go for it! The first time I jumped off, I honestly felt like I was falling for 5 minutes. I remember thinking, "Where the hell is the bottom? Why haven't I hit the water yet? Aaaahhhhhhh!" And then *Splash*! I made it! What a rush that obstacles was. Once it was over, and I overcame my fear, I couldn't wait to try it again!

Another tough obstacle was a board that we needed to put pegs in to pull ourselves up and then reinsert the peg into the next hole above it until we pulled ourselves to the top. This one took a toll on our upper body because it was like doing 15–20 slow pullups to reach the top of the obstacle. The obstacles were designed to be both mentally and physically taxing. And they did an excellent job of that!

The temperature for our first three laps was relatively pleasant. Las Vegas was around 50° F with mild winds: great weather for a race like this. But that didn't last long. As Giovanni and I scaled the desert mountains and crawled under barbed wire obstacles, we soon found out that Mother Nature was going to play a significant role in this race.

As the clock hit 5 pm, the sun was basically gone, and the temperature crashed from 50° to about 35° within a couple hours. The wind began to pick up, and as we started our fourth lap, fighting the elements became a real challenge. A couple obstacles consisted of short swims, and the water was frigid. I had a wetsuit on with a thicker wetsuit type jacket over it, but it didn't come close to keeping me warm. However, swimming wasn't as bad as getting back out of the water and into the 30-degree weather. That made my teeth chatter. But even with Mother Nature wreaking havoc, we completed our fourth lap, which was 20 miles total.

During each 5-mile loop, Giovanni and I would meet up with my fiancé, his dad, and his friend to chat about how things were going, stretch out, drink water, and eat something to keep our energy level up and our bodies warm. I didn't want to feel bloated or cramp, though, so I had to be careful about overeating. What a mental, physical, and emotional battle!

Our fifth lap started around 7 pm, and it was pitch black outside, so the only light on the course came from our mini head lamps on our foreheads. Being in the middle of the desert and unable to see more than 20 feet in front of you was ominous. I looked up at the mountain and saw dozens of small specks of light as the competitors continued up and down the course. Other than man-made obstacles, who knew what else could be out there in the dark? After 20+ miles on this course, my mind was making up stories about what crazy critters might be waiting for me to turn the corner and enter their territory. But luckily I had Giovanni there, and our conversations distracted me from my wild imagination.

At one point, though, I had to ask Giovanni, "What do you think my fiancée, your dad, and your friend are doing right now?"

"They are probably all bundled up, sitting around a fire in the Pit, sipping wine."

I laughed. "So true! They have to act like they are concerned about us, when actually they can't wait to shove us off for the next 5 miles."

Giovanni laughed and imitated them, "Are they far enough away yet? Coast is clear. Steph, hand me some hot chocolate and another piece of pie. They won't complete another lap for a couple more hours, so we can relax and catch the rest of the football game."

We both cracked up. I looked over at Giovanni and thought how lucky I was to have him as my friend as we pushed our minds and bodies to the max. It was a blessing to have someone with me the entire time to talk and laugh. If he wasn't there, I'd be doing this race alone, without a fun and inspiring sidekick. I was so grateful that Giovanni found me on social media and we formed this connection.

After a tough, cold, and windy finish to our fifth lap around 9 pm, it was time to refuel and stretch out. The temperature was around 30°, and my body was slowing down. My knees ached, legs were sore, and upper body burned during most of the obstacles we had to complete. However, I was confident that I had many more miles in me. We tried to warm ourselves up by changing our socks, putting on a new pair of gloves, and drying off. The problem was, within the first mile of the course was a water obstacle, so we would be soaked for the rest of the lap anyway. While we were in the Pit, we got word that 20–30 people had already been picked up in an ambulance due to hypothermia since the temperature continued to plunge.

Knowing that some of the top athletes were in the hospital didn't give me a warm, fuzzy feeling at all . I kept thinking that as long as I felt strong enough to continue, and wasn't in any real danger, nothing was going to hold me back from pushing on.

What we didn't realize was that the worst was yet to come.

With freezing temperatures and very limited visibility, we had been surmounting 25+ obstacles over insanely hilly terrain for each lap. But I think I made the mistake of thinking, "How can things get any worse than this?" It had been slightly windy for the last few hours, but as we pushed through our sixth lap—around mile 27 of our journey— the wind became a major issue. It kicked up so suddenly that it felt like a small tornado had just dropped on us.

As we reached the peak of one of the mountains, I looked down at the Pit area. It was the only bright spot on the course because of all the portable lights, but it looked like a tidal wave of sand had just crashed over it. It wasn't any better for Giovanni and I on top of the hill as the sand began blistering our bodies and faces. My face felt like it was getting shot with insanely small bullets as each grain of sand struck me. We both covered our faces as much as possible, but the small grains of sand would always get through.

Giovanni had brought a pair of goggles—lucky!—that he now put on. He told me he never thought he would need them, so it was the last thing he packed in his bag. I, however, had my hand over my eyes as I stared at the ground.

I screamed through the wind and sand storm, "Man, I can't see anything out here! I have to keep my head down because the sand is everywhere! I don't want to hold you back though!"

But then he said, "We've come this far together. Just put your hand on my shoulder and stay behind me. My goggles are keeping most of the sand out of my eyes. I can't see more than a couple feet in front of me so I can't go very fast anyway. Let's keep moving and take one step at a time!"

That is exactly what we did. We took one small step at a time and kept pushing forward. I was nervous for my wife and Giovanni's crew in the Pit because we could see the wind blowing tents all over the place. It was mass chaos down there. After the race, my fiancé said she was so nervous for us on the course during the sandstorm, when it was basically the two of us against Mother Nature.

The howling wind and sand made talking pointless for Giovanni and me, so I was basically left to my thoughts. I tried to stay focused on the reason I was doing this event, and the amazing woman I had just proposed to a couple days prior. But then thoughts would creep in like, "Who goes out in the middle of the dessert to do an insane event like this? I'm freezing, I'm crazy, and I need to just get back to the Pit and get out of here!" But that doubt wouldn't own me tonight! No way. I was out here for such a bigger reason than myself, and I would push myself to the breaking point for it.

It was past midnight as we slowly pushed toward the finish line on the sixth lap. The ambulance was extremely busy driving from the Pit area to the nearest hospital. Hypothermia was becoming the norm as each competitor fought to stay as warm as possible. Actually, being warm was not possible. We all fought to stay the least freezing that we could.

As Giovanni and I stumbled over the finish line on our sixth lap, we officially completed our thirtieth mile! The wind was blowing at nearly 50 mph, the temperature was 24° F, and I could barely feel any parts of my body. Every time my foot hit the ground, my knee felt like someone was pounding it with a sledgehammer. Both knees were in excruciating pain and my whole body was numb from being so cold and wet. We were over 14 hours into the race, and it was time to decide if we could take any more.

Steph looked at me nervously as we walked side by side into the hospitality tent where over 100 other competitors were attempting to warm up enough to try another lap on the course. I wasn't sure if I could continue. My body was shutting down, my limbs were frozen, and my knees were on fire with pain. That is when one of my life's defining moments happened. This moment was so profound and intense that I can close my eyes now and feel every emotion.

Giovanni, his dad, his friend, my fiancé, and I all stood in a circle inside the hospitality tent, and nobody said a word. All of us were thinking the same thing, though: we were wondering if Giovanni and I would attempt another lap considering the weather and how terrible we felt. Finally, I broke the silence. "Well...?" was all I could muster as I looked over to Giovanni. He looked back at me and put his head down. Then I, too, lowered my head to my chest.

That's when I read those four letters that were half covered with mud on my chest: "YACS." I was doing this event for young adults in Pittsburgh, Pa., who were battling cancer.

These people had their whole lives ahead of them before being blindsided by a terrible diagnosis and forced to leave work or suspend their schooling. They battle each and every day and, for the most part, do it with a smile on their faces. They smile in the face of cancer. For years these young adults fought, and as I looked down at that race bib, I knew I could fight another 5 miles for them! That would mean thousands more dollars being donated to help them deal with their treatments and possibly improve their lives. How could I give up now when they never did? I couldn't! I looked up at our small circle; got this confident, motivated smile on my face; and said "Let's go, my man! 5 more miles! We got this!"

Years later, I look back at this moment and know that, had I been doing this event on my own, solely for my benefit, I never would have done more than 20–25 miles. But doing an event that I knew was so much bigger than me motivated me to complete another 10–15 miles in the worst sandstorm Las Vegas had seen in over 20 years!

Giovanni nodded, and off we went for our seventh lap. I won't lie to you. About a mile into that seventh lap, I may have regretted my pep talk forcing Giovanni to keep going. The weather refused to let up as sand continued to pelt us like paintballs while we pushed on. In fact, the weather became a much tougher obstacle than any of the man-made ones were. One massive 30-foot wooden structure actually blew over due to the high winds. Nobody was injured, but it was scary seeing such a obstacle just lying across the course. We slowly walked around it and continued on.

The situation out in Las Vegas that night was brutal and indescribable. I could only think of the YACS group to help get me through the seventh lap.

Giovanni stumbled across the finish line, which was barely visible, to complete 35 miles. Giovanni's dad and his friend were already holding their tent that they had packed up and were ready to leave as the clock approached 2:30 am.

My wife, the trooper that she is, said, "If you want to continue, I'll stick it out with you. I'm here for whatever you need. I didn't clean up yet because I know you, and I don't want to make that decision for you."

I looked at her with a mud-filled smile. "I can honestly say I've pushed my body as far as it will safely allow me to go. I told myself I wouldn't stop unless I couldn't go any further, and I don't think I could do one more mile right now. My knees are on fire, I'm absolutely freezing, but I couldn't be happier with what we accomplished! I love you so much. Let's pack up and celebrate!"

*****

What an experience!

I learned so much throughout this whole process. I learned that life is so much bigger than one individual, but that one individual can create a huge impact for many by having a vision and clear goals and not stopping until that vision is lived out! My vision for this event started over a year prior to taking on this course. A vision just starts out as an idea, and some might say in my situation, a crazy idea. But then, with a plan in place, the vision starts to take shape. I began to train, and I started getting people to sponsor each mile that I completed. Slowly and steadily, this vision became a reality.

I never had such a clear vision about anything before this event. I had dreamed about playing college basketball when I was growing up, but I never put a plan together for making it happen. With the World's Toughest Mudder, I visualized my goal actually happening and put all my energy and enthusiasm behind my vision. Visualization needed to become a part of my morning routine after the World's Toughest Mudder because that's when I clearly saw how powerful visualizing things can be.

Not every vision will happen exactly as we see it in our heads, I'm sure, but this one turned out even better than I could have imagined. No, I didn't plan on a massive sandstorm hitting that night. But I did visualize the pledges coming in for YACS, my wife going crazy over our engagement, and me pushing myself to the point where I truly felt I could not continue. I gave it my best! I visualized leaving it all out there on the course, and that's exactly what happened.

We raised almost $15,000 for Steph's Young Adult Cancer Support group with this event, and it all started with a vision.

Doing this event also taught me about gratefulness and helped me recognize how lucky I was to be able to put my body to the test like I did. Before, I sometimes took for granted that I'm able to lift weights, run outside, or do crazy fitness events. But not anymore. I considered myself the luckiest person on the planet, and being grateful for every moment and every breath was something I had to implement in my morning routine too.

I thought about how lucky I was after this event was over. I had healthy lungs, a great heart, two arms, two legs, and a brain that was back on my side as my confidence continued to rise. I also was lucky enough to meet the woman of my dreams and ask her to marry me in Las Vegas. We created memories of a lifetime over that long weekend and I couldn't have been more thankful for that.

I was also thankful for the people who supported me and YACS through donations for this event. It didn't matter if someone donated a thousand dollars or $10 because people gave what they could. Miracles happen constantly in this world, and most of the time we never hear about them because they are overshadowed by negative news stories that we are overexposed to. This World's Toughest Mudder event was a miracle. I was and still am so grateful for people being selfless enough to give to young adults who were in dire need of the money.

I needed to be grateful each and every morning from this point on. I didn't want to just be grateful for big things like asking my wife to marry me and World's Toughest Mudder events either. That was easy to be grateful for. I also wanted to be grateful for the small things in life, because a lot of the time those are actually the big things. I needed to be grateful for breathing clean air, being able to afford a car, and many other aspects of life that I had been taking for granted.

If I lived in a grateful state, then it would erase a lot of stress or fears that I had in my life. It's impossible to be grateful and stressed out at the same time. It's also impossible to feel grateful and fearful at the same time.

As it stood, my morning routine was already extremely positive, uplifting, and powerful. But it didn't have much focus on being thankful for what I was blessed with, relationships I had, and other things that helped me become the man I was. It lacked gratefulness. I was so grateful for this World's Toughest Mudder experience because it helped me gain an even stronger sense of purpose for what I was put on this Earth to do. That purpose is to help individuals that aren't able to help themselves.

I hoped a gratefulness practice would help me become more selfless, kind, and at peace with everything and everyone around me. The Tough Mudder was a beautiful experience that helped me add a new life-changing practice to my morning ritual.

*****

Current First 15:

5 minutes—WAKE UP! "Yes, I get to play again!" Stretch, water, water, snack.

2 minutes—Goals. Review/update goals!

2 minutes—Grateful Greatness. I learned through the World's Toughest Mudder process that I need to be grateful for everything I have in this world. We can't be great without being grateful. It took a huge event for me to understand how important it is to be grateful. But more importantly, I learned how crucial it is to be grateful for little miracles that happen to us all the time. We all have hundreds of things to be grateful for, and having a gratefulness practice would help me realize both large and small aspects of my life that I could appreciate more.

How to do it: Sit comfortably, with your back straight and shoulders back. Put both hands over your heart: this will help you get into the grateful state, feeling it within your heart. Think about three things you are grateful for, and truly feel the energy in your body as you pour everything you have into your gratefulness. What you think about can be extremely simple or more complex. It's up to you. As you do this, keep taking deep slow breaths, and enjoy this practice.

2 minutes—Power Visualization. I started planning my participation in the Tough Mudder in 2013, and the event was in November 2014. This event made me believe that when you visualize something and see it through in your head, anything is possible. ANYTHING. The power of visualizing is absolutely amazing and incredible. So this had to be something I added to my daily routine, and I think you need it in your morning routine also. Visualizing crushing something that you feared is a huge confidence booster. Each morning I visualize myself in the near future, and distant future achieving massive success involving something that I want to conquer in this world.

I also learned that doing something nice for other people made me feel more alive than ever! In this situation it was raising money for my wife's YACS group, but it doesn't have to be something big like that. I wanted to start doing something small but very nice for someone every day. It doesn't matter if you do something nice for a friend, family member, or stranger. I take a few seconds during my visualization practice and picture myself doing something nice for someone during the course of my day. It's been a complete game-changer for me. I consistently do nice things for other people now, and I see myself actively looking for ways to be helpful and nice. It's a whole different mindset that I love and am addicted to!

How to do it: Stand up tall and strong! Visualize yourself having massive success in whatever you are passionate about. Visualize what your goals/dreams coming true would look like, and really see it happening. Visualize the time between now and when you'll drive off to work or whatever the beginning of the day entails. Visualize the workout you'll do and healthy breakfast you'll have. Smile! Then, take a few seconds and visualize one small act of kindness you will do for someone that day. It doesn't matter how small or big the act is, but I think we can make the world a better place, one small act at a time.

Examples of small acts of kindness include smiling and opening the door for a few people that day, sincerely complimenting a co-worker or friend for something wonderful they have done recently, or leaving a larger tip than you normally would to make that server's day!

1 minute—Laugh!

1 minute—Pep Talk!

1 minute—Check social media, read texts from previous night, watch some TV

1 minute—Play upbeat music to get me excited about the workout

Analysis: It was so cool to see how the first 15 minutes of my day was ever-changing but always started in a positive and upbeat way. The worst thing to do is to wake up and do/see something awful like watch the news because it can bring you down. I want to avoid that each and every morning. I also couldn't be happier to implement the Grateful Greatness practice into my morning routine.

Thinking about 3 things I'm grateful for each morning helped me live life in a grateful state. If I could be grateful in good moments, and also in bad times, that would be a wonderful feeling. Adding in a visualization practice each morning also is a huge bonus. I learned how powerful visualization can be. Seeing things happen perfectly before they even occur can increase your chance of success. This also ties into building confidence in yourself when you are entering the unknown. I wanted to increase my chances of a positive result by feeling and seeing myself succeed before it happened.

I continue to decrease the amount of time I watch TV or check social media also. Soon those will be completely out of my morning routine. My First 15 was coming together and getting more and more powerful!

Chapter 8 – Calm your Mind and Become More Selfless

"Only those who will risk going too far can possibly find out how far one can go."

~ T. S. Eliot

The feeling of completing 35 miles in the World's Toughest Mudder competition was incredible and one of the most emotional successes I've ever had in my life. It was a moment of perfection! The mindset and vision I had coming into that event meant everything and was the very reason for my success.

It's amazing that if a person keeps telling themselves something over and over and over, it eventually becomes their reality. That's what I noticed. We are our repetitive thoughts, and we are the stories we make up about ourselves, whether those stories are true.

By the time I finished the Tough Mudder, my reality was completely different from when I started my healthy living journey. I had a much more positive mindset, and I felt like I could do whatever I set out to accomplish. The first 15 minutes of my morning are the very reason for the mindset I had. I felt as if my morning routine and my daily attitude of positivity coupled with massive amounts of energy came from the process I had adopted and continued to improve upon, called the First 15.

I continued to embrace the mindset that I was an insanely healthy, motivated, positive, driven man who was extremely fun to be around while completely sober and being himself! There's my mantra for myself. And guess what . . . combining those thoughts with my First 15 was an amazing 1–2 punch for changing how I saw myself. I began to become my thoughts and my mindset. If I put positive self-talk in my head consistently, then I would become a positive person with a lot of self-worth and self-esteem!

The mind is a complete beast. I love learning how to feed it with the most uplifting thoughts to keep it as strong as possible. It's one of the toughest and most fun challenges I've ever faced, and my First 15 has been the biggest helper for keeping me in a positive mindset throughout my day.

In addition to working on my mind, I began to teach myself to think BIGGER about life, think bigger when it came to my goals with healthy living or in holding a fundraiser. I played small for a lot of my life and was content with thinking smaller. But why play small when you can play big? Why help two people if you can help 20 people? I began to realize my passion and energy for thinking much bigger than I ever had in my life. That is when the idea to set a World Record came about.

My morning routine helped me remove mental blocks that had kept me from thinking bigger. Years prior, if I even thought of something bigger, my mind would say, "What are you talking about Matt? You'll never pull that off. You are too weak to handle that." You know that little person in your brain who likes to come out and put you down? Well, my whole mindset now shifted because of my new fitness experiences and my morning ritual, so the loudmouth Negative Nelly was quiet more often now. That allowed more room for growth and thinking on a bigger scale regarding fitness endeavors, but it also applied to any other challenge.

I was looking for my next fitness challenge in 2016, and I decided to attempt to set the world record for most burpees completed in 12 hours. The current record was 6,800 burpees in 12 hours, which averages to 9.5 burpees a minute. My mind was set on doing anything I could to break this world record.

I started practicing burpees in 20- and 30-minute intervals to see how I would feel. One week I did over 500 burpees in one workout session, then 750, then 1,000, and then over 1,500.

I noticed the way other gym members would look at me as I did burpee after burpee. I imagine they thought, "You do realize there is equipment in the gym right? You don't have to just do burpees right there." I couldn't help but laugh at myself after some of the quizzical looks I received.

After 4 months of intense training, my body was strong enough to do burpees for 3 hours straight. I was taking 2–3 minute breaks every hour to use the bathroom, rehydrate, and get some calories in me. This is when things took a turn for the worse.

On my first 6-hour session of burpees, I was moving along just fine, when my lower back gave me a little jolt like it was saying, "Matt, why are you making me do hours and hours of these? Stop!" I ignored my body for a few minutes to see if I could work out the problem. I was 4.5 hours into the training session when pain really began to set in. I was frustrated because I really wanted to accomplish this goal, and I had a great training plan all figured out, but the pain in my lower back told me I had to stop. No world record is worth damaging my back.

Clearly, I learned the importance of listening to my body during this world record attempt. In today's society, we hear a lot about pushing yourself through any sort of pain no matter what because pain is weakness leaving the body. I completely disagree with that. I think being a little sore and feeling some burn in your workout is great and essential to building muscle. However, being in pain and actually feeling like something is wrong with your body means it's time to stop and evaluate what is going on. Please listen to your body because it will tell you what's going on. And if pain lingers for a while, don't wait until it gets much worse or becomes a long-term issue. Get checked out and make sure everything is ok.

Listening to your body is important during workouts, but it is also important with our food intake. How many times have you been full but, because you still see food on your plate, you feel obligated to eat the rest? I'm guilty of this from time to time for sure. Listening to my body has helped me know when I'm full and think about how I'll feel if I keep eating. I already know I won't feel good later if I keep eating now, so that motivation helps me stop. Or, when you get full, you can practice smiling and pushing your plate away so you connect smiling with the feeling of being full and the empowerment of pushing the plate away once your appetite is satisfied. Connecting smiling with pushing food away will actually help you feel amazing. Bottom line: listen to your body! It knows what to do.

But after listening to my body and ceasing to train for the burpee world record, I felt like 4 months of training went to waste. So I changed my mindset. I told myself that the time spent training wasn't a waste because I learned about my body and what I could and couldn't handle. Learning about my body was a positive takeaway, and this setback wasn't going to stop my desire for another intense fitness event.

Maybe I could find another way to challenge myself. The old Matt who played small and gave up quickly wouldn't have been open-minded enough to keep thinking. Endurance burpees weren't my thing, as my body clearly told me. But maybe there was another avenue I could take to break a world record. My new fitness and life motto became, "Always happy, never satisfied!" I was always happy and grateful for the life I had but never fully satisfied because I always wanted to keep growing and moving forward.

My first 15 minutes of each morning told me not to give up and to keep looking for a new, aggressive goal to achieve. After researching for weeks, I finally found a world record that looked possible for me: the 1,000,000 pound world record. A man in Russia was able to lift 1,000,000 pounds in just under 10 hours by only using four upper body weight machines in the gym. The machines were the bench press, military press, lat pull down machine, and low row machine. I love all four of these machines, AND I love lifting very low weight with high repetitions. So this 1,000,000 pound world record would be perfect for me! This would be a true endurance test. I couldn't wait to begin training!

No more than a month after failing in my attempt to do 12 straight hours of burpees, I was on a mission to lift 1,000,000 pounds in less than 10 hours with only my upper body on those four machines. My wife Steph could only laugh as she wasn't surprised by my addiction to continue to see how far my body would safely allow me to push it.

As summer 2016 turned to fall, I started spending several hours in the gym once a week to see how much weight I could lift. I had contacted a man with Guinness World Records so he could tell me what I needed to do to prove I was attempting this world record.

I couldn't believe how well the training was going. My failed burpee world record attempt helped motivate me to push myself on this record. And it helped! My workout sessions went from 1 hour to 2 and then up to 4 hours. That's when I realized . . . 10 hours is a long time! What food I would bring into the gym during my workouts also became an ongoing joke with my wife because I had to fuel up each hour I was lifting weights so my muscles and body wouldn't give out.

I enjoyed all my training sessions: it was fun to push myself further and further. I also learned the value of setting specific goals throughout this process. I had used a goals spreadsheet in years past, but this event really helped me plan out what goals I needed to hit and in what amount of time I needed to hit them. I was on pace to go for my world record attempt, which was supposed to take place on November 4th, 2016.

Every morning, I would check what goal weight I needed to complete that Saturday. I did all of my world record preparation on the weekends because I knew I'd be in the gym for hours and hours. Seeing my goals written out each morning when I woke up helped me keep them fresh in my mind and realize that they were possible. Realizing that I was hitting each and every goal as the months of training moved on was so important to motivate me.

Unlike with the burpee record, my body was holding up just fine for this World Record attempt. I got up to 500,000 pounds in the gym in about 4.5 hours, so I figured if I could just double that on game day, I would break the record. I knew my body would fatigue and I wouldn't be able to do the second 500,000 pounds in 4.5 hours, but that was ok. I needed to break 9 hours and 55 minutes to set a new world record.

I felt well prepared as my last long training session ended two weeks before the big day! I like to let my body rest for a while before leading into a huge event like this. Even with a triathlon or obstacle course race, I like to take a few days off before the event just to let my muscles and body rest up.

My body was ready, so I began to train my mind more for this endurance challenge. My wife and I had attended an incredible mindfulness event at the University of Pittsburgh that was perfectly timed with my training ramping up. I learned about calming my mind and gaining more control over my thoughts, and I wanted to use this new knowledge as I trained for hours in the gym. I knew my physical strength was only half the battle. My mind would have to keep me focused, calm, and ready for any minor setbacks that may happen.

Meditation is an excellent way to learn about controlling your mind, and there are many ways to practice meditation. I suggest learning about a lot of them and then choosing which form works best for you. I use a deep breathing technique while sitting with good posture, eyes closed, and soft music playing as I let my thoughts go. When a thought would enter my brain, I would slowly let it float away and remain focused on my breathing.

If you've practiced meditation before, you know the feeling you get during the first few attempts at this practice. Your brain wanders and comes up with some crazy and silly thoughts. After sitting in silence for a few seconds, weird thoughts would enter my mind like "I wonder if it's cold out," or "I need to use a Q-tip in my left ear," or "I wonder how many more *Star Wars* movies they will make?" and then "I'm not even sure how many *Star Wars* movies there are right now." My job was to just keep letting these crazy thoughts go and return to my breathing.

The benefits of meditation are backed by science and include reducing stress, improving concentration, increasing happiness, and slowing the aging process. I figured I could use all of these as I attempted to lift weights for hours and hours. For me, practicing meditation absolutely helped me remain calmer and more focused on my 3–4 hour long training sessions. It helped me concentrate on the current repetition I was doing and not let my mind think things like, "There's no way I can do this for 6 more hours," or "Oh my goodness 1,000,000 pounds is so far away!" I knew adding meditation to my morning routine would be a must after seeing and feeling the benefits of it throughout this world record process.

Have you ever tried meditating? I challenge you to give it a chance. Try it for one or two minutes in the morning, and concentrate on your breathing.

On the day of the world record attempt, the four machines I needed to use were basically off limits in the gym, so I had free rein of the equipment. My wife came with me and rolled a large cooler into the gym. It was full of the fuel I would need for this attempt, and she absolutely got some funny looks.

Steph had to send thousands of pictures and hundreds of videos to the team that tracks world records to validate my record because the committee decided not to send anyone onsite during the attempt. The gym owner also had to set aside some time to watch me because a fitness professional had to validate the world record, as well.

My strategy for the attempt was to do 50 pounds with each repetition on each machine. I would rotate which machine I used and would do 20 repetitions on each machine for a total of 1,000 pounds per set. Completing 1,000 sets would get me to 1,000,000 pounds. Hopefully, that would be exactly how it was executed. All I had to do was 20,000 repetitions of 50 pounds, and boom, I'd be sitting pretty at 1,000,000 pounds. That simple, right?

Right before I started the attempt, I did some deep breathing and visualized myself holding up the plaque that said "World Record" on it. I also repeated a pep talk to myself: "I AM going to be a world record holder today! I got this!" I knew that if my mindset was extremely positive and I believed in what my body could do, then anything was possible!

The First 15

I started my attempt and was quickly able to get over my nervousness because I knew this was a major marathon of an event and not a sprint. The first 5 hours were a blur. Everything went as planned with my food, water, fuel, stretching, and pace. The pace was actually almost too fast as I had completed 600,000 pounds in 5 hours.

But it wouldn't be fun without any curveballs. I suddenly felt like my body was talking to me like ground control in *Apollo 13*: "Matt, we have a problem." My right forearm was becoming more and more painful because of my hand constantly gripping the machines, and the strength in my hand greatly decreased. That's when I wasn't able to grip the lat pulldown machine in any way that didn't bring excruciating pain to my right forearm.

I didn't worry too much because I was now 650,000 pounds in and I could still use three machines. Well . . . that didn't last long either. At about 675,000 pounds, my shoulders began giving out. I had been doing 20 repetitions of 50 pounds each on the shoulder (military) press, and at this point, I couldn't do more than 3–4 repetitions without dropping the weight.

There I was, with over 300,000 pounds to go, and I was down to only two machines. It was getting close to midnight, since we started at 6 pm. I grimaced at my wife. "That's it. I can't do shoulders anymore. They have given out." Then I chuckled. "How exciting is it that I'm still able to do bench press and the low row machine?" We both laughed. The attempt wasn't over because I could just use the only two machines left for the next 300,000 pounds. And that's exactly what I decided to do.

I attribute my ability to complete the next 300,000 pounds absolutely to my First 15. Because of my morning routine, I had become mentally strong enough to overcome many obstacles. I had reprogrammed my brain to overcome adversity when I was faced with it instead of crumbling. I had put together strategies like my pep talk, breathing exercises, and meditation to get myself through this intense endurance challenge. These strategies and my mindset kept me going.

It also helped that the only brother I have in this world paid Steph and I a visit around 1 am. It was a very welcome surprise, and the timing was great because it was a long night and Steph could certainly use someone to talk to as I just breathed heavy and went from machine to machine. Seeing the two of them talking and laughing made my heart warm, and it took the pain off of my entire upper body for a few minutes. (Note that I was in pain, but I knew I wasn't injured.) I started to get excited, too because each rep got me 50 pounds closer to my ultimate goal.

My brother left around 1:30 am, and other than Steph, the bench press became my world because it was the only machine I could do that wouldn't put me in severe pain. My muscles were still painful as they were stretched well beyond what they had ever done before, but my training propelled me forward as the clock ticked close to 9 hours into the challenge.

Steph couldn't believe it, and I was absolutely in shock. If I hustled, I could complete the World Record attempt in less than 9 hours! I could potentially break the previous record *by a full hour*! We tried to stay calm, but the owner of the gym even got a little excited at this point. He was to remain impartial, but it was almost 3 am, and I'm sure part of his excitement was because he wanted to get home.

Only 10,000 pounds to go.

Then 5,000 left.

1,000 to go!

Only 5 repetitions left.

It is so crazy how the mind works sometimes. As my wife and I counted down the last 5 repetitions of the world record attempt, so much went on in my head. It was as if the last 10+ years flashed right before my eyes. I caught glimpses from my functional alcoholic days. I thought about when I cried as I began my quest to make positive changes to my life. Moments like winning Mr. Pittsburgh, asking my wife to marry me, and doing the World's Toughest Mudder all flashed before me as the countdown continued. I felt so fulfilled and accomplished. It was euphoric! I was about to be A WORLD RECORD HOLDER! WOOOOOWIEEEEEEE!

As we counted down, the celebration began. The official time completed was *8 hours and 58 minutes*! I had done it! I lifted one million pounds using only those four machines in under 9 hours! What a crazy feeling! It didn't feel real!

Once the attempt was over, I realized that I had learned so much about goals, mindset, and my body that I could pass on to thousands of people in the future! This attempt wouldn't mean anything if it was all about me. It's the ability to use this knowledge to help others push through barriers or break through obstacles that they never thought were possible! That's where I get my joy from!

I certainly didn't get any joy from the recovery because I had to take a month off from lifting weights because of my forearm pain. I wasn't able to squeeze anything with my right hand and shaking hands with someone else was painful. The funniest part was struggling to hold a fork because I couldn't grip anything with my right hand. In case you want to try it, I challenge you to eat an entire meal with your non-dominant hand. I bet you'll laugh at yourself like I did, but I was so frustrated that I considered smashing my face into the plate and sucking all the food down my throat. Lucky for my wife, I didn't put her through watching something like that. You're welcome, Honey!

After completing this world record at 3 am Saturday morning, November 5th, 2016, I used that momentum to springboard myself to the next challenge. What was next? I wanted to lift 1,000,000 pounds using only the leg press machine! My contact at Guinness World Records actually challenged me to do that next. What started out as a simple joke, turned into another 2.5 months of training and another world record attempt on January 29th, 2017. On that day, I became the first man on the planet to lift over 1,000,000 pounds in less than 7.5 hours using only the leg press. I did it in 7 hours and 13 minutes!

I had to pinch myself as I lay in bed after the leg press world record—I mean, after I took two Epsom salt baths, used a foam roller for an hour, drank a gallon of water, and iced down my thighs, of course. Then I had to pinch myself because I never would have thought 5 years ago when I was drinking ten beers a night that I would soon be a back-to-back world record holder for lifting 1,000,000 pounds. I had conquered my drinking problem and knew with 100% certainty that I could never have another drink in my life. I felt so incredible and powerful just knowing that was a fact now. I didn't shed any tears this time, but I did have a huge smile on my face as my head hit the pillow that night.

Before dozing off, I gave thanks to the good Lord who clearly had a huge hand in pushing me through all of this. Not only was he there during both of my world record attempts, but God helped me completely turn my life around. Within a few years, He helped me so much and was with me through it all. I smiled up at Him and prayed and thanked Him for watching over me. I also apologized to God for blaming him years prior for my problems with alcohol.

Then I started thinking about the times I pray. I usually only pray when big events are coming up or if someone close to me is going through a really tough time. I also admitted to myself that the majority of my prayers were for me. I would often ask God to watch over me during a fitness event or help me get through a difficult time. I wanted to become more selfless and use the power of prayer to help other people I cared about.

I was so happy that I realized this after setting these two world records. I couldn't have been happier with my accomplishments, but I learned that being selfless and gearing more of my prayers towards others would be very helpful. It was something else I wanted put into my morning routine.

My parents always told me to say a prayer before going to bed, but it was something I never got into the habit of doing. Come to think of it, my parents gave me a lot of advice that I should have listened to. One of those pieces of advice was to be careful with alcohol at college, and clearly, I should have listened on that one, too. Now, I planned to set aside 1–2 minutes each morning for prayer.

That night, I thanked the good Lord for giving me the gift of my wife, who was an unbelievable supporter and especially because she never complained about it being late or that she was tired. I also thanked God for my brother showing up and for all the support my parents and family gave me—not only my side of the family, but Steph's side of the family, too. The people who supported my efforts on social media provided me with a boost throughout the night and also leading up to the big event, so I gave thanks for them, too. I truly felt like the luckiest guy in the world with all this support.

I never realized all the miracles in my life in my drinking days. But now that I was sober and living my best life, I realized that small miracles happened every single day. I just had to notice them . . . and give thanks for them.

The other thing I noticed as I prayed that night was that as much progress as I had made with the mental aspect of my life, I was guilty of starting to pray for others and then letting my mind get sidetracked. I needed a better way to stay focused on my prayers while I was praying.

I came up with an idea. I know that I enjoy moving my body, and I concentrate better when I'm moving. Moving helps me focus my emotion and even create more emotion. So I sat up in bed and held my hands above me as if looking up to heaven and pulling God's power down to me. As I did this, I thought about the person or situation I wanted to pray for as I breathed in deeply. Then, as I slowly exhaled, I pressed my hands out from my body as if to push the prayer to that person or situation.

After trying this once, I was convinced it was a much better way for me to pray because I could fully concentrate on my prayer. From now on, I would use this technique and make prayer a part of my morning routine. Plus, I know my parents have to be happy to read this part of the book because I finally listened to you two! Thanks for the advice, Mom and Dad! It only took me a short 30+ years for your wisdom to sink in!

After thanking God again for my fitness abilities and adding in a few more prayers for family, close friends, and others who needed help, I fell asleep with a smile on my face.

*****

Current First 15:

5 minutes—WAKE UP! "Yes, I get to play again!" Stretch, water, water, snack.

2 minutes—Goals. Review/update goals!

2 minutes—Grateful Greatness

2 minutes—Visualization

2 minutes —Active Prayer/Meditation. Meditation was paramount to my success in both world record attempts so I know it has to be something I practice each morning for at least one minute. Sometimes, I get so into it in the morning or after work that 5–10 minutes will pass without me even realizing it. It can help to set an alarm on your phone to keep track of how long you've been meditating.

Praying is something I had done sporadically in my life before, but now, it was an essential part of my morning routine. I feel amazing when I send a few prayers out to people each morning.

How to do it: For both Active Prayer and meditation, I sit on the floor with my legs crossed, back straight, and in a comfortable, strong position. Then, I sit for at least 1 minute in complete silence (or with calm music playing) and focus on my breathing (diaphragmatic breathing—this type of breathing is explained in Chapter 15) or a guided meditation.

Follow this with 30–60 seconds of praying for up to 3 people in need and sending love to others. Focus on the person and say a nice prayer for them. Put your arms above your head as if reaching for the sky as you slowly breathe in, and then push that love and prayer toward the person you are thinking about as you slowly breathe out. The Active Prayer will help your mind stay on course and focus on the prayer. Remember: motion creates emotion.

1 minute—Laugh!

1 minute—Pep talk!

Analysis: I'm very happy to have finally cut out social media and TV in the first 15 minutes after waking up. I feel wonderful being 100% productive right after getting out of bed without getting sidetracked. I decided to cut out playing music in the morning because I knew when I hopped in the car to head to the gym, I could play upbeat music then.

Meditation helped improve my mind, my focus, and my stress level leading up to the world record attempts. In realizing how important meditation was to my success, I knew it had to be something I implement each morning. Now, meditation can help me with other parts of my life.

The addition of Active Prayer has been wonderful, as well. It helps keep my mind on others and create a more selfless mindset first thing in the morning. I also noticed that I forgive people much sooner because of my Active Prayer practice. I often pray for those who have given me a difficult time in the past and hope for the best for them.

The addition of Active Prayer and meditation has helped my morning routine improve in a great way as I continue to tweak the First 15.

Chapter 9 – The Invention of the Smile File

"The two most important days in your life are the day you are born and the day you find out why."

~ Mark Twain

What a journey life took me on from October 2011 until October 2017 (when I wrote this chapter). It blows my mind to think about how a life can change so much in 6 years. I'm humbled, excited, and more energized than ever because of the last 6 years. I'm also more motivated than ever because I've uncovered a major purpose in my life. That purpose is to take all of my experiences and teach others strategies to conquer their mind and body. A major part of my purpose was writing this book. It's one thing to become motivated, but to remain motivated, it's important to know your true purpose. Then it becomes a habit that never goes away.

I feel so blessed that I've been able to change my life. Those changes have allowed me to become Mr. Pittsburgh, be on *America's Funniest Home Videos*, and be featured on *American Ninja Warrior*. I've completed tons of Spartan Races, Tough Mudders, and the World's Toughest Mudder. I have enjoyed half marathons, triathlons, and 100-mile bike races. And now I can say I'm a two-time world record holder. I'm the luckiest man on the face of the planet for being healthy enough to achieve all of that.

I owe all of that success to the people I surrounded myself with and my morning routine. It is that simple. As my lifestyle changed, so did my group of friends, and they lifted me higher than I ever thought possible. I found my true self and was able to meet the woman of my dreams. My morning routine continued to make me feel energized each day, grateful for what I had, and motivated to keep moving forward. I got to the point where I thought, "Now what? What's next?"

I still compete in fitness events and always want to keep pushing myself in healthy living endeavors, even when I'm in my 80s and 90s. However, my greatest joy now comes from giving back all of the knowledge and experience I've gained through my good times and bad. I want to share them all so others can learn from my many successes and mistakes. I want to help individuals both young and old break through their barriers and become the best version of themselves!

I enjoy doing events like the Tough Mudder and other events that are team-oriented because my excitement doesn't come from when I cross the finish line; it comes from the joy of helping fellow teammates who are completing the event for the first time. When you see someone with a huge muddy smile across their face, knowing they just did something that they feared for years, it is the most rewarding experience ever.

As I dug deep, thinking more about my purpose, I knew I didn't want to be known just as an athlete who had some nice accomplishments. I want my legacy to be one of giving back, sharing my knowledge, and helping change the lives of thousands—or even millions—of people. I want to speak to people about strategies to uncover their true meaning and use that meaning to create the life they want to live. I want to focus on healthy living as a starting point for their change because, if you aren't healthy enough to live your dream, then it will be impossible to accomplish.

I want you to achieve a level of success that fully fulfills you! In my brand, Livin the Dream, "D.R.E.A.M." stands for "Diet, Rest, Exercise, Attitude, and Meaning." After figuring out your meaning and working on your attitude, you can build on that foundation by working on your diet, rest, and exercise. If you achieve a high level of success in all five of these pillars, I believe you will be Livin the Dream!

The next step in my journey had to be to start giving back, so that is why I began studying to become a health coach. After completing the certification, I could supplement my personal experience with facts about the healthy living world. I was a personal trainer for years but that didn't give me 100% fulfillment in changing lives because I was only showing people the best ways to exercise in the gym. My purpose was more than that. I loved learning about my client, their mindset, and how they perceived themselves. I wanted to combine the mental coaching with the physical fitness coaching.

I laughed when one of my health coaching clients, Bill, said, "Matt, you know your little World's Toughest Mudder and world records? They will seem like a walk in the park compared to working with me!" Bill did have a point! My physical challenges were so different from working with people in one-on-one health coaching. But I loved it! Nothing worthwhile is easy.

I love helping people discover their true meaning for wanting to change their lifestyle. Knowing the deeper meaning for why you want to change will motivate you. The best motivation comes from inside of you, not from some external force like a trainer pushing you or a family member staying on you about losing weight. My goal is to coach someone to the point where they don't need me anymore and are internally motivated enough to sustain their healthier lifestyle.

Sometimes when people try to get healthier, they fight the change for a while, almost as if they feel like they are being pushed away from healthy living. Some feel like the only way for them to stay on course is to hang on for dear life. That means it will take willpower for that individual to keep up this change. But willpower only lasts for so long. Willpower is only reliable at the start of any change you are trying to make.

However, once you fully understand your deep reason for change, then you'll feel as if you are being pulled *toward* being a healthier person! Then the changes become real and you win the internal battle! For me, it no longer took willpower to be healthy; it had become a habit, an amazing lifestyle that I craved every day of my life. Once I had this feeling within myself, there was no going back to the old me because I never felt so strong, upbeat, energized, and positive. I guarantee the same thing will happen to you once you find that internal motivation and meaning behind why you truly want to change. This holds true for any change you are trying to make.

After years of training, coaching, and speaking, I have helped a lot of people. I didn't realize the impact I was having on others, though, until I heard from Brad, an old friend from Boston. He wrote me an email stating that he followed me on social media and used my motivation and inspiration to shed over 20 pounds. His relationship with his wife and kids is better than ever!

I was melting as I read this email. It meant more to me than any trophy I won or fitness competition I did because I realized that I had a positive impact on someone's life, and he improved himself because of my impact. This email was one I wanted to read every single day to keep me motivated to help others on their personal development journeys.

I printed the email and began to look at it 3–4 times a week. Every time I read his words it brought a huge smile to my face and hit an emotion that I loved. I wanted to eventually have 10,000 emails like this so I could impact people across the country! But why stop at 10,000? I wanted 10,000,000 emails like this so I could help change the world to make it a better and healthier place! Emails like this helped me realize that my purpose was being fulfilled, and I was helping effect positive change in people!

Shortly after I printed this email, I began to receive similar emails, cards, text messages, and social media messages from clients, as well as random people who were inspired by the energy, passion, and excitement I was bringing to their lives. I printed out all of these positive messages from anyone who told me I helped them because these interactions helped me understand my meaning, and they also kept me extremely motivated to continue to help others.

I gathered all of these correspondences in a folder and wrote "Smile File" on the front of it. This file was something I NEEDED to add to my morning routine. This file is something that I beg you to start right now because it is an essential part of a higher quality of life! I wanted to look at one of these amazing messages right after I woke up every morning. The Smile File is a perfect way to remind yourself of how amazing you truly are and how many lives you've touched.

I know helping people become healthier and reach their potential is my main purpose, and seeing the impact I've had on so many people helps me understand that I need to keep going after my life's mission no matter what setbacks occur. This Smile File is the perfect tool to have whenever you've had a bad day or worked with a difficult individual because it'll pull you right back into feeling amazing and understanding the truth about how incredible you are!

*****

FINISHED First 15:

The First 15

3–5 minutes—WAKE UP! "Yes, I get to play again!" Stretch, water, water, snack.

1 minute—Smile File. When I first started making a Smile File and feeling the love from people I had an effect on, it was so addicting and such a simple but beautiful practice! It is NECESSARY to do this! You need to know how awesome you are, and this will give you proof every day! I challenge you to have a positive impact on someone and then continuously remind yourself of that impact! It . . . is . . . LIFE CHANGING!

How to do it: Make a folder where you put all of the positive comments, compliments, or appreciation that people have sent you. If someone writes you a note about something great you've done for them, put it in the file. Maybe the note just says that they love you. You helped change someone's life? Great! Put that in your Smile File! If it's in an email, text, or social media format, print it out and put it in the file. It HAS to be emotional to you, and it helps if it's tied to your meaning/purpose in life. If it's tied to your purpose, it will make you feel joy and excitement as you read each morning. Read ONE a day! EVERY DAY! THIS might be the most important part of the morning routine because the Smile File keeps you directly tied to your purpose every time you open it up! It also shows you how awesome you are and the impact you have on others!

1 minute—Goals. Review/update goals!

1-3 minutes—Grateful Greatness

1-3 minutes—Active Prayer/Meditation

1-3 minutes—Power Visualization

30 seconds—Laugh!

30-60 seconds—Pep Talk!

Then go work out!

Analysis: I had finally done it! After years of trying to figure out which routine worked best for me in the morning, I found it! This was such a wonderful feeling as I knew I had a strategy in place that I could use each morning right after I woke up so I could attack the day. This is a life-changing morning routine that I will commit to doing each day of my life. The only thing better than doing this morning routine every morning is sharing and teaching others to use this strategy to conquer their own morning!

The other awesome part of the strategies inside the First 15 has to do with the combination of the Smile File, Meditation, and Visualization. Think about the order of those three practices. The Smile File focuses on achievements in your past, meditation helps keep you in the present, and visualization will encourage you to see an amazing future for yourself! Goal Setting will also help with that. You have past, present, and future all covered within your morning routine! I think this is a huge factor in the power behind this incredible habit!

Section 2

Analyzing the First 15 Routine

The First 15

3–5 minutes: Wake Up!

1 minute: Smile File

1 minute: Goals. Review/Update

1–3 minutes: Grateful Greatness

1–3 minutes: Active Prayer/Meditation

1–3 minutes: Power Visualization

30 seconds: Laugh!

30–60 seconds: Pep Talk!

Go work out! Or bring on the day!

Chapter 10 – First 15: YOUR Life-Changing Habit

"Successful people are simply those with success habits."

~ Brian Tracy

Thank you for taking the journey with me through the ups and downs of the first 34 years of my life. One of the major things I've learned is how important the first 15 minutes are to each and every day you wake up! They are HUGE. They can shape the day you will have, and in turn, they can shape the life you will have. I believe that because my life is a perfect example of one that completely changed because of my first 15 minutes each day.

Journaling in the morning had a profound effect on my life. Reading those journal entries in my alcoholic days made me examine my life and helped motivate me to change. Deciding what will help motivate you to change is important because it will be different for everyone. I don't know you, and I don't know your challenges. What I do know is that you will benefit from a bunch of the strategies laid out in the First 15! As long as you carve out time for yourself each morning and make it consistent, you will see wonderful results in your life.

No matter what you select to include in your First 15, block out the first 15 minutes of your morning *at least* five days a week, and do your routine. You can get plenty of negativity throughout the course of a regular day, so to combat that, make your first 15 minutes as positive, fun, and energized as possible! Some mornings, you may meditate longer. Some mornings you may feel like journaling longer. And that's ok. Having a productive 15-minute morning routine is paramount to your success as an individual, as a family member, a teammate, an employee, or an entrepreneur.

You may be married or have kids, dogs, or other responsibilities in the morning, and that's great! But, I think it's even more important to get your day off to a positive start with a family at home because you clearly want to be at your best for them each and every day you are alive! Children have a ton of energy and your First 15 will help you stay energized through getting the kids ready for school or playing with them on the weekends. It will help you stay more positive around your family and be less affected by any negativity that may surround us at work or at home. Make your morning routine a top priority in life!

If you absolutely cannot figure out a way to carve 15 minutes out of your morning, that's ok. In that situation, I recommend giving yourself 5 minutes each morning. And don't BS me. We can ALL create an extra 5 minutes in the morning, even if it means setting our alarms 5 minutes earlier than normal. Take 5 minutes and do your favorite two or three pieces of the First 15. I recommend, at the very least, looking at your Smile File every day! Commit to this 5 minutes for 30 days! No excuses! Make the commitment!

Then, after a month of having your first 5 minutes down, add another 5 minutes, and work your way slowly up to 15 minutes. I do believe it is essential to eventually get to 15 minutes in the morning because I've seen it change so many lives, and I know it can help change yours too! As you complete each First 15 (or First 5 or 10), you could make a checkmark on your calendar to let yourself see the consecutive days you've accomplished your morning ritual. This is a way of habit tracking, so you can visually see the commitment you are making to this routine. This is one way to hold yourself accountable for your morning habit.

Another way to hold yourself accountable is to share this routine with a family member or friend and do the First 15 together. Or at least check in with each other each day to make sure you are both staying on track. Having an accountability partner is a wonderful way to stay on track with any change, as long as that accountability partner is as committed as you are. If not, then that person will slack off and try to get you to do the same. Make sure you are very selective when it comes to an accountability partner.

Please remember that my life didn't change overnight and neither will yours. Sorry to burst your bubble if you thought that may happen. I'm a very positive person, but I'm also realistic. Any change takes at least 30–90 days to become a habit, and this routine is no different. Once this First 15 is a habit, your confidence will increase, you will feel more grateful for the life you have, and I bet the smile on your face will be even bigger throughout the day! But give it time.

It also doesn't matter what time you wake up. I understand you may not get up and have a 9–5 job, and that's perfectly fine! Whether you get your 8 hours of sleep and wake up at 6 am, or you get 8 hours of sleep and wake up at 2 pm, all that matters is that you start your first 15 minutes of the day in the right way!

I noticed so many changes once I gained control of the first 15 minutes of my day! I NEVER crash at work or at any point throughout the day, and I have more energy than I've ever had in my life. I used to be a zombie between 2–4 pm before I changed my lifestyle. But, after conquering my first 15 minutes of my day, I now float straight through until the end of the day when it is time for bed.

I often get asked this question, "Matt, do you ever sleep? You have more energy than anyone I've ever seen." I always laugh and say that I have more energy than you've ever seen because I probably sleep more than anyone you've ever seen. The energy I have doesn't happen by mistake. When you get quality sleep and wake up with a purpose in the morning, your day is going to zoom by! You will also be more productive, and you'll have more energy than you've ever had in your life.

As I write this book, I am 34 years old, and I promise you that I have more energy than ever while being in the best shape of my entire life. I've never had endurance like I have now, nor the strength or mental toughness. I'm also on the go much more than I was back in high school.

My favorite part of this 15 minute morning routine is the fact that I feel much less stressed because of it. The stress relief happens due to a combination of strategies. Getting enough sleep and eating a healthy breakfast are two great ways to help tame stress. Also, meditation and prayer combined with a morning workout are huge ways to decrease stress.

Simply having a more structured first 15 minutes of your day will make you feel like you have so much more control over the rest of your day. Conquering the First 15 will boost your confidence levels throughout the course of the day and help you to take on any challenges that may arise.

Getting 8 hours of sleep is so crucial to becoming healthier, being more productive, and making better nutrition selections. When I don't get a lot of sleep, the following day is usually the most challenging because I always want to reach for a coffee, some sweets, or something sugary that will help me plow through the day. Those are direct reactions to being tired. When you get 8 hours of sleep, the chance that you make poor food decisions decreases significantly because you'll be more alert and focused on your healthy living goals.

Another issue with not getting 8 hours of sleep is the endless cycle it can create. When we don't get enough sleep, many of us reach for caffeinated beverages throughout the day. Most experts suggest not consuming caffeine after 2 pm because it disturbs our sleep that night. However, when we are tired, we reach for caffeine at 2 pm, 3 pm, or even 5 pm anyway, and it hurts our chances of falling asleep quickly when we eventually get to bed. In turn, this has helped increase this country's over-consumption of sleep medication.

As a society, we have to stop the endless cycle of not getting enough sleep, using caffeine to keep us awake all day, and finally using sleep medication to help us fall asleep. I haven't even mentioned mood yet. We all know that we become more moody or negative after not getting enough sleep for a night or two. Let's avoid that by getting enough winks!

I understand that some people work multiple jobs while also trying to raise a family. I respect you guys so much and applaud your willingness to grind every day because you love them. I understand it may be impossible for you to get 7–8 hours of sleep. If you are in this category, I can only say to try your best to get as much rest as you can. I'd also suggest focusing on a strong five minute routine in the morning and then using the other concepts in the First 15 throughout your day when you have some time.

Over the next 7 chapters, I want to share the 8-step process I like to call the "First 15," which has helped create massive change in my life as well as hundreds of others that I've coached! Plus, this process completely changed who I am and 100% saved my life. Since I quit binge drinking in October 2011, I have attempted to perfect a 15-minute formula that you can use in your own life to help create change, conquer worry, release stress, and gain a healthier mind and body. I hope you start slow but eventually implement the majority of these practices into your own life. It doesn't take long, it isn't complicated, and it works!

Another question I get often is, "Matt, why didn't you incorporate working out as part of your First 15?" I love working out and it's definitely a highlight of my day and something I feel everyone on the planet needs. But to work out effectively, you must first get your mind in the right place. The body is a slave to the mind. I've seen countless people who are in great shape but aren't grateful for what they have or are actually depressed because of other things wrong in their life. I'm sure you know someone who is wealthy but also extremely miserable. That isn't success. To feel and look your best, start with your mind and your morning routine. That is why I chose to focus less on exercise with this book and more on mastering your mind, attitude, and meaning first thing in the morning.

One other question that often comes up is, "How do you make sure you are staying within the 15 minute time limit?" You can accomplish this in many ways. One method is by waking up and immediately setting an alarm on your phone 15 minutes later than your alarm went off. You have to be careful to not set two alarms in the morning because I don't want anyone snoozing through the first alarm and waking up 15 minutes later, thus missing out on your routine.

Another way to maintain your time limit is to play a 15-minute YouTube video of soft music. When the video ends, you know it's time to finish your first 15 minutes routine and go out and crush the day! Or set an oven or microwave timer, and when it goes off, it's time to attack the day! Just choose the one that works best for your situation.

I only use music for the 6–8 minutes that I'm doing my Grateful Greatness, Active Prayer/Meditation, and Power Visualization techniques. I play a soft song that allows me to know when those 3 segments of my First 15 are complete.

I think a large part of keeping yourself within a 15-minute window is just by jumping in and trying it as soon as you are done with this book! It won't always be exactly the same, and that is perfectly fine! Once you get a feel for how long each piece of the routine takes, then you'll be able to better gauge how the timing is going. It will come naturally to you after about a month and will just become part of your daily development practice.

A morning routine is something that needs to be practiced to have the most fulfilling life possible. If you are unable to complete your 15-minute routine in the morning, then all of these steps and strategies can be used at any point throughout your day. That is the best part! If you are stressed out at work, take 5 minutes to sit down and mediate while concentrating on your diaphragmatic breathing (this type of breathing is explained in Chapter 15). It will help you lower your stress levels.

I understand if you can't just sit in your cubicle at work and look like a nut as you meditate, so I'd suggest walking to your car to do it. Or you can sit in the bathroom and do it. Find a place where you can find some peace and quiet for a minute or two, and use one of these strategies to get yourself mentally ready to conquer the rest of the day!

In a sentence, the First 15 will help you live life on YOUR TERMS and have a life full of purpose and fulfillment. With that, enjoy the concepts and ideas behind the strategies of the First 15!

Chapter 11 – Step 1: Wake up!
3–5 Minutes

"Each morning we are born again. What we do today is what matters most."

~ Buddha

Isn't it funny that step one of conquering your morning/day/life is to actually wake up? But it is true! This is arguably the most difficult step of them all. The amazing concept of actually hearing your alarm, opening your eyes, getting your butt out from under the covers, and putting your feet on the floor could be a book in itself.

I've come up with a process that worked wonders for me and has worked for many people I've trained over the years.

First, you have to spring out of bed as soon as the alarm goes off, put your arms up in the air and say, "YES! I'm alive and get to play again!" I like to add a fist pump or mini jump when I do this to wake my body up and let it know it's GO TIME. I believe springing out of bed as soon as the alarm goes off is also important because your brain doesn't have time to stop you! Your day HAS BEGUN as soon as you stand up! Why does it make sense to put your arms up and say you get to "play again"? "Playing" is a light-hearted word that immediately makes you feel like it's going to be a fun day.

We may not feel like doing any number of tasks in our lives, but if we turn them into a game, they usually are much more fun to perform. The statement "I'm alive and get to play again" makes life feel more like a fun game, and it'll make you feel grateful to be able to participate in that game again. After all, the alternative to being alive isn't nearly as appealing, so give thanks as soon as you wake up. Being able to live another day in this world is a wonderful gift.

A lot of older people say, "Every day above the ground is a good one." I've said this phrase thousands of times in my life, and most of the time, it is met with laughter because I'm only 34 years old. But I truly mean it. How can I not be thankful to wake up every single morning when my feet hit the floor? I get another opportunity to pursue my dreams and attack another goal every morning! That is the most amazing feeling ever! Plus, I'm blessed to have a roof over my head and be able to sleep in a comfy bed. I also get to sleep next to the love of my life and wake up next to my best friend every morning.

Every single day is a journey in itself, and I want to make the most out of every one of those journeys. None of us knows how many days we have left on this planet, and I refuse to take any of them for granted. Knowing that tragedy could strike any of us at any moment only drives me to live life to the fullest even more. Waking up with emotion and energy is the only way I'll ever suggest to wake up every morning!

Another key to your morning success is to make sure you are not hungover from the night before. Having a productive and positive morning is difficult if you wake up with a pounding headache. I don't need to discuss this concept in detail because you've seen the downward spiral of my life due to being hungover more than 50% of all my mornings. Please use my story as a reason to not let it happen to you. This routine helped me overcome alcoholism, and it can benefit you no matter what addiction you are struggling with.

You can still have a successful First 15 Routine if you have a drink or two in the evening. But, I suggest limiting it to two drinks if you want to feel good the following morning. In my opinion, feeling your best means limiting yourself to 0–1 alcoholic beverages in a night.

As I mentioned previously, to wake up refreshed, you need at least 7 hours of sleep. I've interviewed many people about their sleep patterns and reasons they aren't getting enough sleep, and a few reasons stick out. One reason is because their thumb continues to search for entertainment after bedtime. They either keep the TV on too long, sometimes searching through channels with the remote, or play around on their phones aimlessly into the night. As this is happening, your body is begging you to just go to bed. This is why scheduling your sleep during the work week is beneficial.

If I know I'm getting up at 6 am and the TV is on at 9:45 pm, then I shut it off ASAP and get ready for bed. My rule of thumb—pun intended—is to shut off all electronic devices a minimum of 15 minutes before you hit the sack.

Another big reason people stay awake longer than they need to is because of social media and electronics in their bedroom. If you have a TV in your bedroom, that is sleep suicide! It's that simple. There is no reason to have a TV in your bedroom unless you want to ensure you never get a good night's sleep. If you have one in there, I suggest moving it to a different room because the bedroom is for sleeping! Ok, and one other thing, but this is a family book.

I have strong opinions not only about social media before bed but social media in general. We discussed earlier that you are the average of the five people you spend the most time with, and I believe the same is true for social media. If you follow 5 or 10 highly negative people on social media, you'll start to become more like those people. It's a slippery slope, so I'm very careful who I follow on social media.

Social media scrolling before bedtime is a huge sleep disrupter, mostly because someone on our social media feed is bound to post something that gets our blood boiling. The worst thing you could do right before bed is to see one of those posts and get yourself all worked up. Plenty of studies show that becoming agitated before bed is not a good way to fall asleep quickly.

I used to follow a ton of people on social media, and if they posted something I didn't like, I would make a sarcastic comment in the thread. Sometimes it became a childish war of words that would keep me up thinking about what the other person said. What a waste of my life! I only did it a few times but that was a few times more than I should have.

Put the phone away a minimum of 15 minutes before bed. And that goes for texting too. I used to sleep in bed with my phone, and that was a terrible decision. I'd be texting my friends until late at night, and I sabotaged good sleep because of it. Not smart. Having that bright light on and close to your face could lead to many health complications also. I now know that sleep is much more important than social media or late night texting about nothing.

Make use of the "do not disturb" feature on your phone before you hit the sack so texts or phone calls don't wake you up. You can set it to automatically turn on "do not disturb" at 9:30 every night and shut off "do not disturb" at 6 every morning. Use whatever your sleep schedule is to determine your "do not disturb" times. You can set your close friends or family members as exceptions on your phone so, if they call because of an emergency in the middle of the night, the phone will still ring. This "do not disturb" feature has been a life saver for many people working on scheduling sleep and making sure they are in bed at a certain time.

If you are having a tough time getting to bed at a decent hour because of electronics, then try setting an alarm 15–30 minutes prior to hopping into bed. When the alarm goes off, turn your phone on silent, and put it face down on your nightstand or dresser. As soon as it goes face down, that's it. You are done with it for the night. And if you want a little extra "oomph" in the morning, set your phone so you can wake up to a song you love. Most smart phones will allow you to do that. I have 4–5 different songs that I love to wake up to! I switch songs weekly to keep them fresh and fun.

One other problem to avoid is setting multiple alarms on your phone! Don't do it. Unless you truly want to get into poor sleep habits, that is. If you have multiple alarms set, we all know you aren't going to wake up until the final alarm goes off, so just give yourself one option for your alarm. I remember asking a client I was training what time his alarm was set to go off in the morning. He replied, "Which one?" Which one? Oh boy. Only set ONE alarm in the morning!

Another key to your morning success is leaving your alarm clock or device across the room. If your alarm is within arm's length from your bed, then shutting it off or hitting snooze as soon as the alarm goes off will be too easy. Put your alarm clock somewhere else so you'll need to stand up and walk over to turn it off. By the time you wake up, walk over to the clock, shut it off, and stretch a bit, you'll be awake and hopefully get your day started much easier! That's when you announce "Yes! I'm alive and get to play again," and start your First 15!

Another idea that my wife and I started using in 2016 is to not have a bright clock in your bedroom. There's no reason for it. If someone can tell me a good reason why I need to know what time it is when I get up to go pee in the middle of the night, then I'll buy a clock and have it in the room.

What happens when you wake up in the middle of the night? You check the clock right? Then you do sleep math to calculate the maximum amount of sleep you'll get before your alarm goes off if you fall back asleep right at that moment. It's a complete head game. If you don't have a clock you can see in the bedroom, you will never have any idea what time it is when you wake up, and you won't care! Then you won't be stressed out if it's only an hour after you went to bed or if your alarm is set to go off in 45 minutes. None of that will matter to you, and as a result, I bet you will fall back asleep much quicker! Try it!

After you have yourself all woken up from giving thanks, getting enough sleep, and not being hungover, you must do the stretch, water, and water routine.

Do a quick stretch like touching your toes, and hold it for a few seconds to wake up your joints and your muscles.

Then drink 8–12 ounces of ionized water. Ionized water is an amazing way to make sure your body's pH is balanced in the morning. Many studies have shown that alkaline water and a more alkaline diet in general can help fend off illness, give you more energy, and potentially defend your body from more serious diseases. Pouring a glass of water and squeezing some fresh lemon into it has a similar effect, so give either one a try first thing in the morning.

Also, since your body hasn't had any fluids all night due to sleeping, it's a perfect way to hydrate as soon as you wake up. I'm not completely against coffee, but I am against drinking coffee first thing in the morning. The reason is simple: coffee will dehydrate your body, even though it gives you that caffeine boost. If you wake up already partially dehydrated because you haven't had water in 8 hours and the first thing you put into your system is coffee, your body will become even more dehydrated. Not the best way to start your morning.

If you are a coffee drinker, I recommend drinking at least 8 ounces of water in the morning before you start sipping that caffeinated beverage to avoid starting your day in a dehydrated state.

The second "water" in our process is to throw very cold water on your face in the morning. This is an awesome discipline, and while it doesn't sound pleasant, it'll help you wake up and give you a nice jolt early in the morning. I don't mean any of this "some cold water and then a little bit of warm water" either. Oh no. Don't wuss out. It has to be freezing cold water to get the full benefit of this discipline. I also love finishing my showers with cold water because it is a huge energy boost. It is a tough discipline and helps me conquer my mind. It is also good for your muscles if you have just worked out in the morning.

Making yourself do something like dousing your face with cold water first thing in the morning is a great way to get your brain to work for you! Our brains aren't designed to help us do things we don't want to do, so you just have to force yourself to do this. It'll help you take on a tough task first thing in the morning and better prepare you for other tough tasks you may face throughout the day.

My client Jason described the cold-water-on-your-face discipline like this: "This is by far the thing I look forward to the least in the morning, and it's by far what feels the best after I've done it." He understands that he has to get his brain to do what he wants! Conquering this discipline each morning provides him with confidence to handle so much more throughout his day.

125

The First 15

After the water, and depending on what your day consists of after your First 15, I recommend a quick snack (I love a banana first thing in the morning) so your body understands that it will be put to work a little later with a nice workout.

That's it! You've conquered the first 3 to 4 minutes of your morning! Now onto the part I love the most, which is making your Smile File!

Chapter 12 – Step 2: Smile File

1 Minute

"A smile is a curve that sets everything straight."

~ Phyllis Diller

If you only do ONE thing that I suggest in this book, please make this the one! Having a Smile File is the most important concept that I teach and will probably be the most unique thing you hear. It is necessary for you to have the most fulfilled and amazing life!

If you truly want to be happy in this life, then happiness needs to come from within you, not from external factors. Think about it. If your happiness comes from the weather, your mother-in-law's mood, or how your sports team did and any of those three aren't perfect, then you won't be happy. That isn't fair to you or your health! YOU DECIDE when you are happy. You control your attitude! This Smile File will make it much easier to wake up and CHOOSE happiness instead of becoming a victim of your circumstances and letting external people or events control your happiness.

You NEED to have a folder (or really nice binder like my wife got me) of good things that happen SPECIFICALLY TO YOU. Did you receive a great email, text, or social media post? Make sure you capture it and print it out. It goes in the smile file. If someone pays you a huge compliment in a big meeting or even one on one, write it down, and put it in the Smile File. This is a very personal file that will help you keep your head up during tough times and show you how much you mean to this world! It's an insanely powerful tool that is crucial to your day, especially during tough times where you don't feel valued. This will change all of that!

Another example of something to add to your Smile File is something that you overcame in the past. If you were nervous about a big project or tough presentation but you ended up doing a great job, add that to the Smile File! This file will help you manage your memories and have clear evidence of amazing things you've conquered in the past.

You could even write down how you felt after you did well on the project or speech. That becomes a confidence building memory you can pull strength from for your next project or speech, instead of any memories that aren't as uplifting. When we are assigned a big speech or presentation, a lot of us start thinking about past experiences we had in the limelight. If you have a few excerpts from your Smile File that remind you of your success in front of others, then read those excerpts and remind yourself how awesome you are as a speaker!

You NEED to read one segment of the Smile File each morning. Building a substantial Smile File may take a while, and that's ok. If you only have 2-3 things in your folder for a while, just keep reading one each morning to keep you going. Yes, you'll read the same email, comment, or text message a bunch of times, but that's ok because it's special and shows you why you are a wonderful human being! Reading about how awesome you are won't get old, right?

If you only have a few excerpts in your Smile File after a month or two, then I have a challenge for you. Make a point of going out and making a difference in someone's life that day! Then, see how that person reacts, and put it in your Smile File. Take 30 seconds to hold the door for people walking into a coffee shop. Help someone struggling to carry their groceries to their car. Tell someone how much you appreciate them, and smile sincerely as you do. Any small act can change someone's day and will be a perfect addition to your Smile File so you can be reminded every morning how much of an impact you had on that person.

As you progress in creating your Smile File, it will become easier to think of things to add to it. You'll start looking for emails or cards that make you feel fulfilled to add to your Smile File because this morning ritual will become addicting due to the positive affect it has on you!

My wife started her Smile File a while ago, and she loves it! It's so fun because if Steph comes home and mentions something great that happened at work or in her personal life that day, she will immediately say to me, "You know where this is going, right? Oh yeah, adding it to my Smile File!" She has built up a nice Smile File and now looks for more ways to have positive impacts on people's lives. It's beautiful because it not only changes the person's life that you touched, but it also changes us in such a profound way.

Why does the Smile File work? It hits EMOTIONS and changes your state immediately. As you read amazing things people have said about you or personalized reports of your success and the impact you've had on the world, you'll begin to stand up taller, you'll clearly be smiling ear to ear, and it puts you in a peak state first thing in the morning! It also helps build confidence in yourself because you can see all the different positive ways you have impacted people's lives.

Why is the Smile File so important? The Smile File makes you feel so worthwhile and appreciated first thing in the morning! It shuts down any negative chatter with proof that you are an awesome, amazing person. What better way can you start the morning than by feeling like you have a purpose and are fulfilling that purpose?

Will you have a much better day, no matter what you do, if you pump yourself up in the morning and feel appreciated? You better believe it!

I coached Marissa, who swears to me that her Smile File helped her understand her worth in this world and opened her eyes to the positive effects she has had on so many people. She told me, "This Smile File idea has become such a habit to me now. I can't wait to wake up, and I get so excited because I'm not sure what amazing thing I'm going to read about myself until I open that file! I used to feel depressed often but now that I use this tool, I see myself differently, and it has had a huge impact on my outlook on life!"

If you have a tough time getting up in the morning, once you train yourself to know you'll get to SMILE first thing in the morning, don't you think it'll be easier to wake up? Your mind will know that, as soon as the alarm goes off, you get to read something that makes you smile and feel great!

This Smile File also works if you are having a tough day and need something to cheer you up. What do we usually do if 19 people give us great feedback on something we did, but one person tears us apart? We feel bad because of the ONE person out of 20 people—95% of the feedback was great, and we let one person ruin the experience for us. The Smile File doesn't allow our minds to do that to us because it only reminds us of the wonderful feedback we received in the past.

You can also put things in your Smile File that you have done for other people that made them smile. That is an example of you making the world a better place! Did you volunteer at a food pantry? Include a note about how you felt during and after the experience. Did you donate money to a cause that is close to your heart? Write about how you felt after doing that. The Smile File is your evidence of the positive changes you make in other people's lives.

It doesn't matter what age you are, what background you come from, or where you live, the Smile File is something every person on this planet can benefit from. Also, when you wake up each morning with a smile, you are training yourself to smile more and will most likely wear your smile more often throughout the day. An old Chinese proverb reads, "Use your smile to change the world. Don't let the world change your smile." This powerful strategy will help you continue that smile throughout your day because you'll see evidence of your worth, you'll know you are appreciated, and you can see how awesome you are each morning in your Smile File!

For one minute each morning, read 1–2 pieces that you have collected in your Smile File. Then, feel the energy and love as you relive an amazing moment in your life. Remember how that moment made you feel, and feel your heart warm.

I believe this is the single MOST IMPORTANT minute in your morning. It will be even more important if you 100% commit to feeling the way you felt whenever this event happened. It doesn't matter if what you are reading was a big event or small moment in time. It made you feel great about yourself, and it is clear proof that you are an incredible human being! Feel yourself smile from ear to ear. What a perfect way to start your morning!

Chapter 13 – Step 3: Goals
1 Minute

"All successful people have a goal. No one can get anywhere unless he knows where he wants to go and what he wants to be or do. "

~ Norman Vincent Peale

Following the Smile File in the morning routine, it's best to review your goals. It's the perfect transition from Smile File to Goals because the Smile File focuses on what amazing things you have already accomplished for others. The Smile File focuses on the past, while reviewing your goals focuses on what incredible things you will accomplish for yourself and others in the future. What a powerful combination!

Growing up, I would always joke with my family that one of my main goals was to write down my goals. Well, it didn't happen until I turned 27 years old. Wow, do I wish I would have listened to them in my teens and began a goals list earlier in life. Without goals, life just passes every day with nothing for you to strive for. How can a person continue to develop without anything for them to shoot for? It's simple. We can't.

The acronym SMART helps us with our goal setting. Goals need to be Specific, Measurable, Attainable, Relevant, and Time-bound. Why do you think so many people fail when they say "I'd like to lose a few pounds?" Some people say that for years or even decades. Why doesn't it happen then? Because they aren't setting a SMART goal. There is no plan to achieve that goal and their goal isn't specific, measurable, or time-bound in that example.

A better weight loss goal might be "I will lose 15 pounds over the next 25 weeks by exercising 4 days per week, drinking more water, eating a healthier breakfast/dinner, and getting 8 hours of sleep each night." That is a SMART goal! It is specific (says exactly what will happen and how), measurable (measured in pounds lost over time), attainable (a person can lose 0.5 to 1 pound per week in a healthy way), relevant (it aligns with exactly what I want), and time-bound (25 weeks).

Goals without deadlines are just wishes that'll never happen. Not only do you need goals, but you need them in specific areas of your life. I use a goals sheet that helps my clients set goals in health, family, love/relationship, friendships, interests/hobbies, learning, career, spiritual life, community, and financial. This sheet has helped many people reach goals that they never thought were possible because, now, they look at their goals each morning. To see the goals sheet I use for coaching clients, just visit my website at www.MattScoletti.com, and print it out for your own goals!

I like to set different goals for different periods of time. Some goals I will be able to achieve in less than 6 months, while others are listed as 2+ year goals. When I wake up in the morning, I can read the reasons WHY I keep pushing every single day. Even a simple goal like "I'm going to make the world a better place by saying 'good morning' to at least two strangers every day" is great! Or your goal may be to "Give (specific amount of money) to (name of charity) this year."

I can't imagine life without these written goals. To me, a life without goals is like a car without a steering wheel. I don't want to end up out in the middle of life's highway with my car driving itself. Who knows where I could end up! Don't make that mistake. Write down your goals and make them SMART goals.

One nonspecific goal I had was that I wanted to become more of an expert in all things healthy living. I needed to make it more specific, so I decided to set a goal to get certified as a health coach, personal trainer, fitness nutrition specialist, and mind/body specialist. And guess what? All the goals happened! When I saw my goals written out and a timetable for me to complete them, they became REAL to me and appeared possible for me to achieve. I have all four of those certifications now, and I learned so much through studying and the exams I took for them. SMART goal setting and reviewing those goals consistently will change your life.

Another important aspect of goal setting is to continue to update your goals sheet and to celebrate your successes, no matter how small. If you make one goals sheet at the beginning of the year, and you hit all your goals in 5 months, that doesn't mean you just sit on your rump the rest of the year! Once goals are hit, you must add new ones to your goals sheet. Never stop setting goals, whether you are 20 or 80!

But never, ever add a new one without celebrating the one that was just achieved. I do not care how small the goal seemed to be, you MUST celebrate it when you hit it. It programs your brain to get excited about the journey you are on and to keep pushing for the next goal! If one of your goals is to work out three days a week, then you better celebrate for a few minutes at the end of each week that you reached your goal! And no, I don't mean celebrate by drinking nine beers on Saturday and eating 2 pounds of chocolate cake. Celebrate by writing yourself a note praising you for a job well done. Or go out for lunch one day or watch a movie you've wanted to see. Or just play a celebration song and dance around your living room! That works for some people! And yes, I am one of those people. Just ask my wife!

I'd like to also mention that you should enjoy working for your goals! The journey is what life is all about, and if you don't learn to enjoy yourself along the way, you'll look back and feel like you didn't get enough out of it. If you have a long term goal of paying off your house in 20 years, then enjoy each and every payment that slowly eats away at the principal loan on the house. Don't just get excited in year 20 when you pay it off. Enjoying your healthy living journey is no different. Set lofty goals that are attainable, but always make sure to have fun and enjoy reaching each goal.

Chapter 14 – Step 4: Grateful Greatness

1-3 Minutes

"Some people grumble that roses have thorns; I am grateful that thorns have roses."

~ Alphonse Karr

You cannot be great in this world without being grateful. Money or fame without being grateful equals disaster.

Tony Robbins says that "success without fulfillment is the ultimate failure." I couldn't agree with him more. To be great and to have a wonderful life, you have to be grateful. That is why each morning I practice gratitude within the first 15 minutes of getting up. It doesn't matter what is going on in my life, I can find at least three things I'm grateful for. I'm sure I could find 3,000,000 things I'm grateful for but I choose to focus hard on three of them each morning.

I've had so many amazing experiences in my life, including trips to England; Spain; France; Costa Rica; Italy; Switzerland; Barbados; the Bahamas; Bermuda; Hilton Head; Ocean City, Md.; San Francisco; Los Angeles; Denver; and so many more! I'm so blessed every single day, and I give thanks for that. I'm healthy, have a great family, married the woman of my dreams, and truly feel each morning that I'm the luckiest person on the planet.

I bet if you think about it, you have a bunch of things you are grateful for also. Think about it for a minute. What are you grateful for? Do you have a car? Do you have a place to sleep tonight? Do you have electricity? Did you have money to buy this book? Are you able to eat three meals today? Really think about what you are grateful for because I bet you could come up with hundreds and hundreds of ideas!

I always make sure at least one of my focuses is on something simple with my gratefulness practice, like having ten fingers and ten toes, being able to come home and eat dinner every night, having a roof over my head, being able to laugh, being able to make others laugh, being able to afford a stand up desk, being able to see, or anything else that would be easy to take for granted. I truly focus hard on one of these at a time and fill my heart with the feeling of being grateful.

What's wonderful about this practice is that there are no wrong three things to focus on. You choose what they are! You cannot mess this up! Just remember to truly focus hard on each of the three parts of your life that you choose. Make sure you feel with your heart why you are so grateful for whatever the focus is and know how blessed you are to have it. Also, be specific in what you are grateful for because it feels more real and heartfelt. The more specific you are when thinking about what you are grateful for, the more powerful the practice will be.

During my Grateful Greatness practice, I prefer to sit comfortably on the floor, sometimes with light music playing, and push both my hands against my heart. It helps me feel my heart beat and feel the emotion of being grateful as I focus on my three things. Try it like this yourself. This technique helps your heart and brain become unified, which you can actually feel as you train yourself to do this each morning. When you can feel it, smile.

This is such a powerful tool to make into a habit immediately! It is especially powerful if you had a bad night the night before or if you aren't excited about something going on during the current day. It puts into perspective just how lucky each and every one of us is.

What I've seen in myself and many of my coaching clients who do this practice is that we have become more vocal about what we are grateful for. After I practiced gratitude for a few months, I found myself telling co-workers, family members, or fellow volunteers how grateful I was that they were in my life. When we train ourselves to live in a grateful state, we want others to know how grateful we are for them.

Even posting something on social media about what you are grateful for is wonderful. A lot of evidence shows that being grateful and expressing gratitude can help with depression and heart problems and even lower inflammation. It seems like a wonderful practice to begin right now!

I'll never forget when my wife and I visited Costa Rica for a long bike event I was participating in. We met a bunch of locals who were the nicest, most generous, grateful people on the planet. They LOVE their country! My wife and I love their country also, but we love it for more than just its beauty. We love it for the beautiful people that inhabit it.

Here's how we knew the people we met were grateful and beautiful inside. One man, Ruben, told me about the day his family installed an actual floor in their kitchen. The rest of the rooms were dirt floors. When his dad put the flooring in the kitchen, he and his two siblings spent every second they were home in the kitchen instead of any other room in the house. He said the first few nights he even slept on the kitchen floor because he was so grateful for it. That is a beautiful state to live in. He could have easily been upset that his family wasn't able to afford flooring in the rest of the house, but instead, he appreciated what he *did* have. Gratitude is an unstoppable force.

Ruben and his country had a huge positive effect on both my wife and me. We live in an amazing neighborhood in a nice house with nice floors, electricity, running water, a garage, and many other amenities. And here's a man who doesn't have 10% of that and is the most grateful person I had ever met. He proved to me that "stuff" can't buy you success. He proved to me that truly being thankful for what you have is a huge part of having success in life. Ruben may not have been set financially, but that doesn't matter. To me, he was one of the wealthiest people I had ever met because of his mindset.

I cherish the day my wife and I were able to meet Ruben and learn from his incredible attitude. In fact, I keep in touch with him to this day. In Costa Rica, the locals talk about living "pura vida," which literally means "pure life." To them, it also means to "live with passion and enjoy every second of life" or "living simply and gratefully are the best ways to live." When I think about living in a grateful mindset, I always think about our amazing friends in Costa Rica and the beautiful state of mind they live in!

Another awesome benefit to having a gratefulness practice is that, when things aren't going your way one day, you are less likely to get upset and stay there. This is because, when you start to get upset, all of the things you are grateful for will pop back into your head, and trivial issues won't bother you anymore. How many people would benefit from this if they knew it would help them not get upset with small things in life anymore? A ton of people! Start your Grateful Greatness practice NOW!

Chapter 15 – Step 5: Active Prayer/Meditation

1–3 Minutes

"Prayer is when you talk to God; meditation is when God talks to you."

~ Unknown

Active praying is one of the most rewarding and amazing aspects of the morning. Whether you are religious or not, you can always pray, wish for someone to be well, or think about someone and send them great wishes. Pray for your spouse, family, and friends and even pray for your enemies because they probably need it the most.

If you are like me, something else jumps into your head while you're praying, and the prayer turns into you thinking about the work day or your pet's next checkup or why your neighbor always mows the lawn at 5 am. To help block out those thoughts, I practice what I call "active praying."

Moving my hands and using my body during prayer helps me think and pray deeper for an individual or a circumstance. Motion helps create emotion, so I use this principle during prayer, as well as many other aspects of life. I sit on the floor (you could definitely do this standing up also or kneeling next to your bed) and hold my hands open above my head with palms facing the sky. I do this as if I feel God's power coming down to me and entering my body and my heart.

I then think deeply about my prayer and the person (or situation) I wish to pray for. As I do this, I pull my hands to my body and interlock them in front of my heart. When I'm ready to release the prayer out to the person, I push my hands forward, away from my body, to send the prayer out into the world and hopefully touch that circumstance and help the situation.

It is a powerful way to remember and feel deeply about who you are praying for and also to keep your mind from wandering to anything else. Each time you pray for someone new, start the process again.

I usually pray for a minimum of three people or three circumstances going on in the world. The whole process takes no longer than a minute and fills you with the Lord's energy and is one of the most empowering feelings ever! Give it a try!

Following my 1 minute of prayer, I begin two minutes of meditation. Many different types of meditation are available, so my challenge to you is to pick one and give it a try. I don't think any type of meditation is wrong, but some types may be better for you than others. Once you find out which form of meditation best suits you, you will feel amazing. Feel free to try many different types before deciding which you enjoy the most.

I enjoy trying different types of meditation, and my favorite is the type where you simply attempt to quiet the mind. Every so often, I'll repeat a mantra or word in my head that helps me calm my mind. As I breathe in and out, I'll repeat the word "tranquility" or "calm" or "peace" because that helps me train my brain to focus on what I want it to focus on.

When I say "calm the mind," that doesn't mean I believe we can stop the brain from having thoughts. I don't believe that at all. I think that's impossible. But we can train ourselves to focus on one thought or one mantra. I try to focus on my breathing and bringing everything back to my breath, while letting random thoughts disappear. If you can accomplish this, then you are becoming a better meditator, which in turn, helps you feel more focused and relaxed throughout the day.

As I sit in a relaxing position, back straight and tall with my palms open and focus on my breathing, it is amazing to feel the thoughts that come into my mind. You'll discover this quickly when you start practicing, too. I enjoy slowing letting each thought disappear as I regain focus on my breathing.

This type of meditation sounds so simple, and it is. But that doesn't mean it's easy. This is a practice that can take years and even decades to master, but I know I have benefitted just by practicing it for a few minutes each morning. My thoughts are more focused, I enjoy the present moment so much more, and I understand my emotions a lot better. I also feel less stress and am able to get much more enjoyment out of life. Meditation is a win/win/win!

One of the women I coach said, "Meditation, even for only 2–5 minutes in the morning, has opened up a whole new world for me. I sleep better, and my thoughts are so much more focused. Thanks for introducing me to it!" This is a perfect example of the wonderful, positive effects meditation can have, even doing it for a short amount of time.

Another person I coach, Greg, said that "meditation helps me discover something new about myself almost every time I practice. It helps me let go of the past and focus on the present moment. I love it and always make it a part of my morning routine now."

Practicing 1–2 minutes of meditation doesn't seem like a lot, but I promise that the first time you meditate, two minutes will probably feel like 30. Sitting in silence (or with light music playing) isn't something that most of us experience daily. That may be why we need it so much. Meditation leaves us with our thoughts for a few minutes and it can be such an enlightening experience.

Finding a minimum of 1–2 minutes a day to meditate is paramount to your success throughout the day and your life! Meditation can help you quiet your mind, organize your thoughts, and become a better and more decisive decision-maker. Also, meditation can help relieve stress, which is quickly becoming the most sought after benefit of meditation.

As our world becomes more busy and technology-driven, meditation becomes even more important. Think about your day. How often do you get to enjoy complete silence? Has it happened in the past few months? Does it ever happen? Our days are filled with "noise" and distractions from children, dogs, emails, social media, co-workers, texting, and so much more. Our minds are being pulled in so many different directions! This is why mediation is so helpful in life. The power of silence is one of life's most amazing beauties and is truly an essential part of a strong morning routine.

Part of what I love about meditation is concentrating on breathing. We don't often think about the way we breathe because breathing is automatic. But breathing is extremely important: it is the first thing we do when we are born and the final thing we do before we die.

Diaphragmatic breathing is a powerful tool that helps balance your nervous system, which will allow the body to function at its best. Like meditation in general, it helps reduce stress by lowering the stress hormones adrenaline and cortisol. Studies have shown that diaphragmatic breathing helps lower blood pressure (lowers risk of heart disease), helps lower blood sugar (lowers risk of diabetes), improves sleep quality, releases serotonin (which makes you feel good!), helps improve your cell health, and improves mental focus by increasing blood flow to the pre-frontal cortex of your brain. How could anyone NOT practice diaphragmatic breathing after reading all of that?!

Learn how to breathe with your diaphragm engaged by first sitting up straight in your chair (or you could lie on the ground with your knees slightly bent) and put your hand just above your belly button. As you breathe in through your nose, your shoulders should not move at all. If your shoulders move during this process then you most likely aren't fully engaging the diaphragm and need to start again. As you breathe in, your stomach should expand, and you should feel your hand being pushed out. That means your diaphragm is being pushed down, which leaves more room for air to fill your lungs.

You can't breathe with your diaphragm, only with your lungs, but you can help move the diaphragm out of the way, leaving much more room for air to enter the lungs. Also be sure to keep your stomach relaxed during this process to allow it to expand and contract easily. Then, as you breathe out, you should feel your stomach contract.

The exact number of seconds you should breathe in or out varies for each individual. I only recommend that your breaths are slow, deep, and relaxed. Ideally, diaphragmatic breathing should be practiced for 3-5 minutes a few times a day, but to get into the habit, it's so important to breathe this way first thing in the morning.

I hope you begin an Active Prayer/Meditation practice right away with diaphragmatic breathing because it can be a wonderful experience as long as you have an open mind and do it consistently.

Chapter 16 – Step 6: Power Visualization

1–3 Minutes

"Imagination is more important than knowledge. For while knowledge defines all we currently know and understand, imagination points to all we might yet discover and create."

~ Albert Einstein

After you have completed your Active Prayer/Meditation, it's time to stand up, get into your power pose, and visualize yourself having massive success! Have you ever been in a situation that went extremely well? It went exactly as you envisioned it might? Of course you have! Part of the reason it went exactly as you thought it might is because you subconsciously visualized the event happening before you even got there. That's what Power Visualization is all about. Visualizing massive success (or even smaller successes) in our lives makes the outcome more likely to occur than if we didn't visualize anything. The outcome will also be much better when you picture something positive happening than visualizing something negative.

Getting into your power pose or "the super hero pose" is an essential part of this routine. I like to stand as tall as I can, feet slightly wider than shoulder width apart, put one hand clenched into a fist over my heart and the other hand down by my side with my palm open. I also make sure my chin is tilted upward. This is just the pose that makes me feel the most comfortable and powerful.

I put my hand over my heart because I always like to feel the heartbeat, and it helps me realize when you do things from the heart, you cannot go wrong. I also keep my left palm open as I stand because

I want to let in and be open to things going on in the outside world and not be closed and defensive.

Another, simpler way to power pose is to stand tall with your feet just wider than shoulder width apart, chin tilted upward, and put your hands on your hips. Putting your hands on your hips and pulling your elbows slightly back will push your chest out further which can make you feel more powerful.

Many studies have been done about what 2 minutes per day of being in your power pose can do for you. The benefits include reducing your level of anxiety, majorly improving your ability to deal with stressful situations, and also helping you boost your confidence. Studies also show that after your 2-minute power pose, you are more likely to take on a risk that you otherwise would have passed on.

This is a great pose to be in as you visualize success each morning. Then, you can do your power pose for 2 minutes before going into a presentation, competition, or high-stress environment (this can be done in the bathroom if needed), and your mind will immediately make you feel and visualize success. The power pose increases your chances of a better performance dramatically.

If you think about the pose, it makes total sense. Imagine trying to visualize massive success as you are slouched over with your head down and breathing irregularly. Clearly, that isn't a great state to be in when thinking about success. Picturing someone trying to think of success in that slouched posture is actually humorous. The way that you manage your physical state in this visualization practice as well as in life is so important.

Imagine standing in a crowded room watching people enter through the main door. The first guy walks in, very shy, shoulders slumped, eyes staring at the ground as he quickly makes his way to a chair by himself. The second guy walks in smiling, standing upright, and walking with a purpose. Which guy has a better power pose or state? Who looks more confident? Who looks more fun to be around? Who looks more successful?

We are making all of these assumptions just by seeing this guy for 3 seconds, and he hasn't even opened his mouth yet! Your physical appearance means so much, so enjoy this visualization practice, because all of us are eventually going to be that second guy walking into the room! Working on your power pose while visualizing your success will, over time, help you become more like that second guy without even thinking about it.

Once you have figured out which power pose works best for you, go with it. Just make sure your back is straight, you are standing tall, your body feels opened up (don't cross your arms because that's a closed and defensive stance), and your head is tilted upward because these are the main qualifications of a strong power pose. Also, smile while doing visualization practices; it might be automatic for you anyway because you are visualizing positive ideas! If not, make sure you get yourself to smile big because you want this to feel as real as possible! And with great success comes huge smiles!

In this pose, take at least 1 minute to visualize yourself having success in life. It could be something in the near future or something in the distant future. Let your imagination run and feel what you truly want in life! If you knew you couldn't fail, what would you want to do? If it's playing violin in front of 50,000 people, visualize that, and make it feel real, as if you are there already. See the people watching you in awe as you play in front of hundreds or thousands. Listen to their applause after each and every song you play. Feel the goosebumps on your skin as you play so well that thousands of people give you a standing ovation!

If you want to become a personal trainer for celebrities, then envision yourself training the biggest stars in the world and truly feel it as if it's happening. See yourself pushing these celebrities as they workout. Visualize the improvements they will make in their strength, agility, power, and mind! Feel your joy as you see them improve with each and every session with you.

If you are trying to get healthier, then visualize yourself having an amazing workout that morning followed by a healthy breakfast. Feel your body getting stronger as you work out on each machine. Feel the increased energy you'll have throughout the day after sweating it out in the morning. See yourself making a healthy breakfast or smoothie when you get back from the gym and taste it. The more specific you make the visualization, the more real it'll feel, and the better chance you'll have of it happening.

I believe that before a workout you should always visualize yourself having an amazing routine and focus on exactly what exercises you are going to attack that day! It doesn't matter *what* you want, it only matters that you visualize in DETAIL everything about the type of life and success you want in this world.

Visualization will also help your creative mind! Watching the news or hearing negative commentary only hurts our view of the world and hurts our thoughts, especially in the morning. I believe the quickest way to lose faith in our country or society is to consistently watch the news. Once I started visualizing more and watching the news less, my mindset completely shifted. I started looking for reasons to like people instead of trying to find reasons why I didn't like them. My paradigm shifted from feeling like people were against me, to realizing that most individuals on this Earth are amazing and most want to support each other. This was a wonderful mindset shift, and one that I will keep forever!

Visualization helps with creativity in a huge way. Remember when you were a kid and thought that anything was possible and you'd let your imagination run wild? We all had huge (and sometimes crazy) dreams of what could be possible in our lifetime. It's time to get back to that, so let your imagination run, and visualize your dreams becoming a reality! Guess what, many people have made their dreams become their reality, and you are going to do the same thing!

I like to visualize myself eating healthy that day, even if I'm put into a situation where there is some unhealthy food present. I actually see the food options and think about making smart decisions and how great I'll feel after eating healthy. The act of visualizing yourself eating healthy and making it feel real will give you a much better chance of doing it once the opportunity presents itself. Visualizing is a form of planning for success in your head and it especially works with meal planning for healthier eating.

Dr. Norman Vincent Peale may have said it best: "Formulate and stamp on your mind a mental picture of yourself succeeding. Hold this picture tenaciously and never permit it to fade. Your mind will seek to develop this picture!" It makes so much sense to see yourself succeeding before it even happens.

Many athletes, entertainers, entrepreneurs, and professional speakers all see themselves succeeding on their respective stages well before they are called upon to perform. If many of the most respected people in the world are all visualizing success before it happens, this proves that visualization is an extremely powerful tool that you should be using.

If you've ever watched a winter Olympics, you'll notice what the best skiers, snowboarders, and bobsled athletes do before their run. Often the cameras will catch the athletes visualizing the track and physically turning and moving their bodies as if they were currently on the course. They do this to see themselves succeeding on each turn and acrobatic move they are about to attempt. Seeing victory before it even happens makes the impossible seem much more possible.

Will Smith, the Hollywood actor, also uses the power of visualization in his life. In an interview, he once said "In my mind, I've always been an A-list Hollywood superstar. You all just didn't know it yet." He said this because he had been visualizing himself succeeding for years and knew it was just a matter of time before we all saw how talented he is. He was right! Will became a mega-star in Hollywood and an amazing motivating speaker to youths and adults across the world.

For years, I had a fear of public speaking, up until my late 20s. Why did I have this fear? I had a few failures on the stage in the past and I would replay them in my head before taking the stage the next time. I told myself a false story. I told myself that I must not be a very good public speaker since I made a couple mistakes early in my life. That wasn't the case at all. This false story and negative visualization killed my ability to give public presentations.

How smart is it to visualize failure right before giving a speech? Not smart! And the reason I failed those 2-3 times in the past was because I would think about how terrible I would look if I screwed up or completely forgot what I was going to say. That's the exact opposite of what you want to visualize! Now instead of visualizing failure, I think about how happy and moved my audience will feel after I leave the stage! Wow, I could have used my book about 10 years ago!

Visualizing success prior to a presentation or speech has helped me tremendously with my public speaking! It changed my life and helped me become much more confident while speaking in public, and I actually love getting in front of audiences as often as I can now.

I went from being petrified of public speaking to becoming an active member in Toastmasters, reading twice a month in front of hundreds of people at church, doing three videos a week on social media for hundreds to see, keynoting many events, and speaking to tons of groups about their morning routine, healthy living, and Livin the Dream. And I do all of these activities completely SOBER! What a change from my past! I owe so much of that success to my visualization practice.

Obviously, visualizing success works with many aspects of life. Use Power Visualization to overcome fears or setbacks you've had in the past, and I guarantee it will help you pushing past your deepest fears.

During your visualizing, after you picture massive success, I challenge you to think about one small act of kindness that you will do that day to give back to the world. You don't have to donate $100 to your favorite charity. All it takes is a simple act like holding the door open for someone else, thanking a co-worker for a job well done, or leaving a waitress a larger tip than you may normally leave.

Visualizing yourself giving back will make it become more natural, and soon you'll be doing one small act of kindness every single day. Giving is a huge reason happy people are so happy. They feel a true purpose in this world when they give back. Take a few seconds during this visualizing practice to decide how you can give back. After it becomes a habit, you'll start finding ways to help people without even thinking about it. That'll make you feel incredible. It'll also make the day of the individual you are helping, as well as anyone witnessing the act of kindness! This can have a huge ripple effect on so many people. That is a beautiful win/win/win.

For years I only thought about myself and didn't go out of my way to help others. Even though I was getting healthier and overcoming my alcohol problem, I thought more about myself. I overanalyzed myself and became too critical. When I started visualizing myself helping others and then following through with it during my day, it helped me stop overanalyzing myself and focus more on helping others. Focusing on helping others also helped my confidence because it feels great to help others. Visualizing the one simple act of kindness will make you a much more selfless, happier, and better citizen.

When I was in New Jersey one, I was walking to a work event and saw some trash on the side of the road. It was right next to the trash can, so I figured I'd pick up a few pieces of trash and throw them away. As I was doing this, a car stopped on the street because the light turned red. The guy in the car was a bigger man and looked like a tough individual. I looked up at him as I was throwing a cup into the garbage can, and his tough looked turned into a huge smile. Then, he gave me a "thumbs up." As I helped clean up a little bit of the street, it put a smile on his face. In turn, I had a huge smile on my face.

I was smiling because I cleaned up garbage. You may have to reread that last sentence because it sounds so crazy. But the real reason I was smiling was because he appreciated what I was doing and I potentially inspired him to do a small act of kindness during his day. I was happy cleaning up garbage. I was happy because I was giving back and doing my one small act of kindness. Don't forget to do yours every day!

Chapter 17 – Step 7: Laugh!
30 seconds

"Laughter is an instant vacation."

~ Milton Berle

Now, you have reached my favorite activity of all time: laughing! At this point in your morning routine, you must laugh! How many times have you heard the saying "laughter is the best medicine?" And it's true! So doesn't it make sense that part of your first 15 minutes of the day should involve taking the best medicine? I think so!

Science supports the fact that laughter is amazing medicine. When you laugh, your brain triggers the release of endorphins, which are basically the body's natural feel-good chemicals. Laughing is also proven to relieve physical tension and stress in your body, which can leave your muscles relaxed for a long time after the laughter is over. Laughter lowers stress hormones, improves mood, boosts immunity, and adds fun and joy to your life.

This morning laugh session will also train you to find things to laugh about more often throughout the day, which will have a huge positive effect on your day. And who doesn't like to be around people who are laughing? You'll become a more joyful person and start to attract more people like you into your life.

Here's another thing, you can't have a good laugh and be depressed or angry at the same time. It's impossible. Think about it. Have you ever been laughing hysterically at something and thought, "Oh my goodness, I'm so upset," at the same time? I bet not. Those two emotions can't happen at the same time. So the next time you are angry over something petty, try finding something to laugh hysterically about, and I bet you'll feel a lot better.

Think about some of your best memories growing up as a child. Think about memories that you have with a good friend of yours. I bet none of those "best memories" were sad. I would guess most of them were positive and a lot of them are flat out hilarious! Doesn't reminiscing with your family or friends about silly or funny things that happened, even if it was years ago, give you the best feeling? Laughing can bring you closer to friends and loved ones, and making laughing a part of your morning routine will help you laugh more often.

With all those benefits, we must laugh during our morning routine. I don't care how you do it, but for 15 to 30 seconds, get yourself to laugh. If you can't think of anything funny, then fake laugh for a few seconds until it turns into a real laugh. If you think this doesn't work, give it a shot; it absolutely works.

I coached Mike for many years. He said, "I never believed fake laughing would make me laugh for real, but it worked. I fake laugh while looking at myself in the mirror to notice how silly I look, and it absolutely helps put me in a better mood to start my day. Now, I do this every day of my life and will never miss a morning."

And if you can, think of something hilarious that has happened to you or someone else and start laughing at that. A third option is to think of a TV or movie line that cracks you up every time. Whatever you use, don't stop until you are laughing out loud! Trust me. It's fun!

I know you could watch a YouTube video clip or turn the TV to the comedy channel, but I don't want you to rely on technology during your First 15. I also know what happens once you watch one YouTube video: you want to watch another one and another one, and before you know it, your First 15 is consumed with watching video clips. Watching funny video clips would actually be more productive than watching the news for 15 minutes, but it doesn't cover all the aspects of your best morning routine and won't help you reach your full potential in life.

Laughter is an amazing tool! Use this tool often! Make sure you get a good belly laugh each morning of your life!

Chapter 18 – Step 8: Pep Talk 30–60 seconds

"Evidence is conclusive that your self-talk has a direct bearing on your performance."

~ Zig Ziglar

Self-talk means absolutely everything in this world. Self-talk can single-handedly be the reason someone becomes a CEO of a company or decides to live paycheck to paycheck, barely making ends meet. Self-talk is the reason someone walks into a room and has all the confidence in the world and is also the reason someone walks into a room and sits in the corner not mingling with anyone. Self-talk is the story we subconsciously tell ourselves about ourselves. We are constantly telling ourselves who we are, what we should do, and how we feel in a situation.

This is where your pep talk comes in! A lot of the thoughts that pop in our heads are negative. Giving yourself a pep talk in the morning will help those thoughts become more positive and uplifting and will help you become much more confident in yourself and your abilities.

A pep talk is one of the most powerful tools you can have. I'm sure you've heard of affirmations and incantations before. Those definitely work and are wonderful! I call my version the pep talk because that's exactly what it is and because it has more emotion behind it than "affirmation" does!

Have you ever seen a football game where one team is down 20+ points going into halftime but comes out and crushes the opponent in the 2nd half? When the star player is interviewed after the game, they frequently give credit to their coach or a player who stood up and motivated the team—aka A PEP TALK! Imagine if, every day, you looked at yourself in the mirror and gave yourself a pep talk, with all your heart behind it...wouldn't it make sense that you'd be more motivated, focused, confident, and energized? I THINK SO! Actually, I KNOW so!

The importance of a pep talk goes so far beyond the positive affects it has had on my life. I give a lot of credit to my pep talk for increasing my confidence and boosting my energy daily. It is when I introduced the concept of a pep talk to my health coaching clients that I saw the major benefits emerging.

John said, "At first, I admit I was uncomfortable saying my pep talk with such intensity to myself in the mirror. Then after a few weeks, I started to enjoy it. And now, 4 months later, I believe every word I'm saying. I've lost over 15 pounds; plus, I feel much more confident in work meetings and in public in general. I learned my pep talk isn't just about weight loss or workouts. I can apply it to so many aspects of my life."

Stacey said, "I never knew how powerful my self-talk was in a negative way. I was subconsciously putting myself down, but when Matt taught me a proper pep talk, I started seeing myself in a whole different way. I couldn't believe the changes I've seen in myself in 4 months, and the majority of it is just trying to conquer the space between my ears."

Erica told me, "My pep talk has been the major difference maker in my confidence level. I pushed back when you introduced the idea because it seemed silly, but now I completely understand why it needs to be a part of my morning routine. I may never totally conquer all of my thoughts, but the way I feel about myself and my self-talk has improved to the point that my friends say I'm becoming a completely different person. I have higher energy and a zest for life now that I lacked before."

Those are just a few of the many examples of people seeing positive changes with their mindset because of their pep talk. So develop your own pep talk that you will use each morning to pump yourself up for the day.

Follow these criteria to make the pep talk as powerful as possible. First, make sure the pep talk is positive. Using negative phrases like "I will not be fat anymore" isn't good. You don't want the word "fat" to be in your pep talk. If your goal is to lose weight, then try something like "I am getting healthier every day" or "I am losing weight and feeling great." Keep the pep talk as positive as possible.

Second, make sure to use the word "I." We are speaking to ourselves, and the most powerful and personal way is to start sentences with "I" instead of "You." It isn't "You are a better coach each and every day," but rather, "I am a better coach each and every day."

Thirdly, make sure your pep talk is in present tense. This is a big one because it makes things happen now—using future tense means these things may never happen. Instead of "I will get better at being nice to my brother," say "I am getting better at being nice to my brother." That way it forces you to act on these talks right away instead of giving yourself an out by waiting till later.

You don't need to be extremely specific in your pep talk. These aren't goals for yourself; they are ways to rewire your brain to think of yourself more favorably. That is all. A pep talk like "I will lose 20 pounds in 4 months" isn't what we are looking for. The issue with these pep talks is, if you check the scale and one week you gained two pounds from the week before, then you will feel like you let yourself down. That's the opposite of what you want to do. You can easily be getting healthier in mind and body, but maybe your weight doesn't change for a few weeks or longer. You want to be positive and keep things in the present tense, so a pep talk like "I am getting healthier" is perfect if you're trying to become healthier or shed some weight. It is in the present tense, it's not too specific, and it is positive. You will believe that statement after using it to pump yourself up in the morning.

Your pep talk also doesn't have to be long. Some people like to have a sentence or two for their pep talk, while others may use a short mantra for their pep talk. Just looking at yourself in the mirror and saying with passion and power "I GOT THIS!" ten times in a row will get your energy up, help you be more confident, and have an impact on your entire day! Plus, saying it with passion will keep rewiring your brain to think, "Oh wow, we *do* have this! We can do this!" and you will have more positive results.

Lastly, you have to exude energy and intensity when you say your pep talk. With motion and energy behind your pep talk, you will strike an emotion and willingness to change inside of you. Your pep talk will have a much bigger impact if it is sincere and intense. MAKE YOURSELF BELIEVE what you are saying! This is crucial! Yes, it may feel weird for a week or two as you deliver this powerful mini talk to yourself in the mirror. But after a while, it will feel essential to starting your day in a peak mental state.

You must state your pep talk at least 10 times when you do it. Saying it 2–3 is good but hammering that pep talk home by saying it 10 times will help you train yourself to truly believe what you are saying and help make you make it happen! These pep talks will push you forward in life and help you understand how awesome you really are! You have the power inside of you to accomplish any goal you put down on paper!

Your pep talk can also be used at any point throughout your day! It is great to use it in the morning to get you excited and confident for the day, but it also works extremely well before a big presentation, competition, or anything else where you might have some nerves. Your self-talk can be the reason you succeed or fail at a particular event or life in general. Keep your self-talk positive and make sure to use your pep talk whenever you need a confidence boost!

Chapter 19 – Pitfalls to Avoid in the First 15

"If you don't build your dream, someone else will hire you to help them build theirs."

~ Dhirubhai Ambani

Now that we have gone through amazing ways to start your day, let's go over some pitfalls to avoid during your first 15 minutes of the morning. I'm guilty of the majority of these over the years, as you noticed in my stories, but I've learned to keep these out of my morning routine because they will pull you down in the morning, not energize you and help you focus. The major pitfalls to avoid are:

Hitting the snooze button or setting multiple alarms. Hitting the snooze button is so 1990s. Today, it's all about setting 3, 4, 5, or 6 different alarms on your phone. That is completely insane to me! Yet it happens all the time to so many people that it has almost become the norm. The sleep you'll get from the time your first alarm goes off, to the time your 5th or 6th alarm goes off, will be unproductive and will not help with your mood throughout the day.

Checking social media. I'm all for social media. It is the reason I've been able to reach so many people with my message! It has been a huge reason that I've stayed motivated and connected to so many people in this country and all over the world. However, social media is addicting. The last thing you need during your First 15 is to be checking Instagram or watching your drunken buddies the night before on Snapchat. Those aren't going to help you get to the next level in your life.

Social media can also bring out emotions in us, and sometimes those emotions are negative. If you see someone post something that offends you within the first 2 minutes of waking up, do you think you'll be able to focus for the rest of your First 15? I know I wouldn't be able to focus. And it could be something as simple as a quote, political comment, or bashing your favorite sports team. Whatever it is, there is no room for it during your First 15.

Turning the TV on. This was my favorite one to do years ago when I first started getting healthy. It just became a habit for me. I woke up, went downstairs, and turned on the TV to ESPN or CNBC. I thought I was getting the knowledge I needed to perform throughout the day or at least entertain myself in the morning. But let's be honest, I could get that same information in 20 seconds by hopping on an app or the internet instead of wasting 15 minutes starring at the tube.

This one could also be a setback because 10 minutes of watching TV can turn into 20 minutes very quickly, and I even missed a workout one morning because I was watching a really good show. I wasn't happy with myself because of it. Please don't let TV get in the way of your First 15 either.

Reading your emails. You have the rest of the 15 hours and 45 minutes that you will be awake today to do this. I don't think anyone needs an email answered in the first 15 minutes of your day.

Checking emails is one of the best ways to get sidetracked from a productive morning. How often have you checked email, seen one you liked, clicked on the link, began scrolling, and then boom, 5–10 minutes vanished? I know I've done it, so I'm sure I'm not the only one.

Even if you get a good email that you want to respond to, by the time you respond, you already ate into 5 minutes of your First 15 when that email could have easily been taken care of later in your day.

Reading emails counts for work emails as well. I'm a firm believer that work isn't a 24/7 thing unless you truly want to burn yourself out or make yourself extremely unhealthy. If you want to stress yourself out, be miserable, and have a tough time spending quality time with loved ones, then make your job 24/7. Otherwise, learn when to unplug, and that means not checking work emails in the first 15 minutes of your day.

We all know that if you see a work email that needs attention, you'll probably take care of it right away. Even if you don't, it will be almost impossible to keep that email out of your mind for the next 15 minutes, which is the most important part of your day, and you need to keep your head in the right place.

Checking your texts. If there were a true emergency, your friend or family member wouldn't have texted you: they would have called. It's so simple to shut off your alarm on your cell phone and then open your texts and check conversations from the night before or read through an entire group chat that your friends were having while you got your 8 hours of sleep.

This was another classic trap that I fell into, but at least at 5:30 am, responding to texts isn't necessary anyway because the majority of my friends and family aren't awake yet. Bottom line: wait until after your morning routine to check your phone for texts.

Turning on the computer. Turning on the computer leads to checking emails, checking current events, and derailing you from having an amazing, refreshing, and energizing start to your morning. Wait until later to check your computer. You have all day for that.

Reading the newspaper. I understand that many individuals need to read the news for their jobs, but STARTING the day this way isn't the best approach. Inevitably you'll read a negative article or something that brings you down, and it'll be difficult to bring yourself back up or forget about that article as you try to conquer your First 15. There's plenty of time the rest of the day to hear about negative news from your co-workers, family, and friends, so don't start your day with that.

Drinking coffee. Coffee is one of the most polarizing beverages ever because when an article comes out about the benefits of coffee, another one will come out the following week about reasons to avoid it. I'm not anti-coffee, but I do ask that you avoid drinking it right after you wake up because coffee doesn't help hydrate you: it actually dehydrates your body. After sleeping for 7-9 hours, your body needs hydration because it's gone so many hours without fluids. I don't discourage coffee in the morning, but I suggest drinking a glass of water before you get your caffeine fix.

Chapter 20 – Other Options to Add to Your First 15

"To live is the rarest thing in the world. Most people exist, that is all."

~ Oscar Wilde

In this chapter, I suggest alternatives to the original First 15 routine that you read about. I make these suggestions not because I think these options are better or worse, but only because I've seen many people benefit from these as well. I believe in altering your morning routine slightly as your life progresses and changes.

Your First 15 doesn't need to be the same every single day. Absolutely not. All I'm suggesting is that blocking out the first 15 minutes of your day for something structured will greatly benefit you, helping change your life in so many ways. If one day you want to meditate for 10 minutes, go for it! If another day you just want to write in your journal for 15–20 minutes because you have a lot on your mind, then do that!

There is no right or wrong way to tackle your First 15 minutes, as long as you focus on YOU! So here are some other options to potentially add in to your morning habit.

Journal. Journaling was one of the main reasons I was able to make a drastic change in my life. I don't journal in the morning anymore, but I always make sure I journal for 5 minutes at night. When I was overcoming functional alcoholism, the best way for me to start my day was to journal. Now, the best way for me to start my day is with my current First 15. However, journaling in the morning is never a bad option.

I also have a gratefulness journal that my wife got for me that I love. I write in my regular journal every night about what happened that day, what I learned, how I feel, or any other random thought I have. Then, I take out my gratefulness journal and write about something that I'm truly grateful for that night. I use my gratefulness journal 2–3 nights a week for a couple minutes. It is a wonderful way to look back and see all the things I'm grateful for, and then I have even more things I can think about during my Grateful Greatness practice in the morning.

Work out! This is always a great option. Some people like to just wake up, drink a glass of water, and jog 3 miles or do some other type of workout. Working out is something I cherish each and every morning, so I like to give myself more than 15 minutes to work out if possible, but if all you have is 15 minutes in the morning(or even 5 or 10 minutes), getting your body moving can have huge health benefits for you over the long haul. My First 15 always happens before my 45-minute workout at home or in the gym. That's just the routine I've adopted because exercising is such an important part of my daily routine, no matter what else is going on in my life. My body is worth it! And so is yours! Make sure you move it daily!

I always suggest moving your body every day, but that doesn't mean you HAVE to do it in the morning. I understand that different people enjoy working out at different times, and that's ok. If you love a yoga or Zumba class that starts at 6 pm, then move your body at that time! Different personality types have different ways of being productive throughout the day, and I completely understand that. I'm not trying to force anyone to work out in the morning (even though it's a great way to start the day), but I *am* pushing you to find time in your day to move your body!

Read The Bible. I don't think this one needs much explaining. I was giving a presentation to a company, and one woman said that she and her family read excerpts from the Bible each morning. I thought that was an awesome idea. No matter what religion you are, there are a lot of valuable lessons to be learned from the Good Book.

Letter to yourself. One of the best concepts I ever heard was to write a letter to yourself. In this letter, you praise yourself for all your accomplishments over the last year, or two years, or however long you'd like to cover. This helps you build confidence in yourself and focus on your successes instead of negatives things.

An alternative is to write a goals-based letter a year before you have achieved something to help it feel more real. So if you are a salesman and your goal for one year is to sell 1,000 phones, then in January of that year, you'd write a letter to yourself 12-months down the road saying how amazing it feels to have sold over 1,000 phones that year. That way, you feel the energy as if it was actually happening.

Watch a motivational video. The only reason I hesitate to mention this one is because if we start using our phones in the first 15 minutes of the morning, ripping ourselves away from them can sometimes be difficult. If you are disciplined, though, sometimes watching a motivational video in the morning can be inspiring and uplifting. YouTube is clearly an amazing resource for this, and even searching for "motivational video" on YouTube will pull up hundreds of videos you can watch to get you excited to conquer the morning and day.

Make your bed. This is a great way to have a productive start to your morning. The military has been using this tactic for many years now for so many reasons. Some members of the military say that making the bed means you've already accomplished the first task of your day. It will make you feel proud and more willing to take on more tasks throughout the day. Taking up this habit also helps you keep the rest of the bedroom tidy, lowers stress/improves mood, and could potentially lead to better productivity, among other things.

Foam roller. I bought a foam roller years and years ago thanks to Chris Johnson's (On Target Living) recommendation, and I use it 1–3 times per week. Many studies show that using a foam roller helps with blood flow to the parts of your body that you use it on. A foam roller can also help release tension that has built up in your body. Give it a shot!

Eat a Healthy Breakfast. Eating a healthy breakfast is something I do each morning after my First 15 and my workout, but if you are truly crunched for time, eating a healthy breakfast could absolutely be a great way to start the first 15 minutes of your morning! Breakfast is so crucial to let your body know that your day is starting, and it helps energize your mind and body to get the day started the right way.

Chapter 21 – Conclusion and Additional Resources

"You were born an original. Don't die a copy."

~ John Mason

Thank you for taking this journey with me! You may be thinking, "What do I do now?" I suggest starting a small morning routine based on what you learned throughout this book. If you can only carve out 5 minutes in your morning, then pick 2–3 disciplines and start with those. As you progress, keep adding more time to your morning routine and slowly feel your life start to change!

I'm not asking for much! All I ask is that you take 1% of your day—yep, about 15 minutes out of the 24 hours—and make it into an unstoppable, exciting, energetic start to your day. If you change 1% of your day, it may just improve 99% of your life. Sound too bold? Reread this book, and see if that didn't happen to me. My life is completely different now and absolutely 99% better! I did it, and more importantly, I've seen it happen to countless other people.

Remember, too, that the strategies outlined in the First 15 can be applied to the rest of your day! All of these ideas work well at any time in your crazy schedule, but the best option is to make them a habit in the morning before the insanity of your day begins. If you think you absolutely can't carve out 15 minutes in the morning due to family, work, or pets, please use these principles throughout your day to decrease your stress and make your life happier and more fulfilled.

I want you to use this routine to realize how incredibly awesome you are! You are an amazing person! I know you are because you wouldn't have picked up a morning routine book unless you wanted to create lasting change in your life. I also know you are the type of person who wants to keep learning about yourself and challenging yourself to get to the next level. And that is BADASS!

This is a habit that takes time to master, sometimes months or longer, to realize all the benefits of it. Actually, it takes longer than that because I'm still learning new benefits of it every time I complete it. I want you to remain patient as you complete and customize your morning routine.

To help customize your routine, head to my website (www.MattScoletti.com) to download a spreadsheet for you to track, modify, and update your routine. You basically build your own morning routine on there to best fit YOU! This will help you see which options you've done in the past and also lets you test out new ones to figure out your best routine.

With patience and persistence, I know for a fact that your life will change by implementing the First 15! I believe it with all my heart and would have never written this book if I didn't believe it. I practice what I preach, and I trust every word on these pages. I do my First 15 a minimum of five mornings a week, and the two days I don't, I typically sprinkle it in throughout the day. It's a part of me and the reason I've been able to feel so fulfilled in my life up to this point.

I know this routine has worked for hundreds of people I've coached. But guess what? Everyone is different and you may be someone who needs to add something totally new to your routine. That's perfectly fine! My goal is for you to create time for yourself for a little bit each morning to personally grow and move toward a more powerful, meaningful life, no matter how you need to do it!

I repeat this routine each morning because I want to continue to think bigger, learn more, and be the happiest and most selfless version of myself possible. I know that sometimes that can take a lifetime to do! I have no problem with that because, as long as we are moving in the right direction, it's a great feeling. The feeling of growth you'll have each morning from your First 15 will keep the fire alive inside of you and keep you reaching for higher and more powerful goals. GO FOR IT! You are worth it! Your body is worth it! Your mind is worth it! Now, it's on *you* to execute this routine and feel all of the amazing benefits of it!

I have a bunch of resources on my website and social media pages that can help keep you motivated, on track, and inspired throughout your journey. Those pages can be found at:

www.MattScoletti.com

www.facebook.com/mattscoletti or just search on Facebook for "Livin the Dream"

Instagram: @MattScoletti

If you follow along on social media, I promise to do my best to keep you motivated and always give you something to smile about. This world already has too much negatively, so I promote the power of positivity, healthy living, and the good things in life!

About the Author

Matt Scoletti has a passion for helping people become more energized, happy, healthy, and productive to live the most fulfilled life possible. His simple, effective ideas and strategies create positive changes in individuals, companies, and non-profits. A certified health coach and fitness nutrition specialist, Matt has been seen on *American Ninja Warrior*, *America's Funniest Home Videos*, and local media as a two-time world record holder. His 15-minute morning routine changed his life for the better as he recovered from alcoholism, and it inspired his first book, *The First 15: The Morning Routine that Took Me from Barely Surviving to Livin the Dream!*

When he's not helping people become the best version of themselves, Matt enjoys spending time with his amazing wife, Stephanie, as well as family and friends. Matt and Stephanie love to travel and have been lucky enough to visit Costa Rica, Italy, Switzerland, Barbados, Australia, New Zealand, and many incredible cities in the United States. They live in Pittsburgh, Pa., where they enjoy trying new things while laughing and smiling through life. They both believe that a day without a ton of laughter isn't a complete day!